# IT'S NOT BECAUSE YOU'RE BLACK

*Addressing Issues of Racism and Underrepresentation of African Americans in Academia*

I0025702

**Annie Smith**

**University Press of America,® Inc.**
Lanham · Boulder · New York · Toronto · Plymouth, UK

# Contents

# Preface

In order to understand the future success or failure of America, it is vital that we examine the current educational state and trends which ultimately means finding solutions to the education disparity in, not only K-12 public schools, but also in higher education. We live in challenging times with an ineffective emphasis on standardized testing and major cuts to education budgets. These times have a tremendous effect on lives, physical and mental health, financial status, and the future of individuals who are interconnected in numerous ways in our society. To some, education is thought to be the *great equalizer.* I once shared that view. Growing up in poverty, I held onto the notion that if only I managed to complete high school, all would turn out well. I truly felt that education would keep me a step ahead of poverty, a place that I longed to escape with no intention of ever returning. But education without opportunity and limited resources keeps the swinging doors to poverty and despair open. Making a decision to recruit or not to recruit African American faculty significantly impacts the lives of students considering attending a university, and impacts students who currently attend. It continues to impact them as they go out into the world and interact with others. This text examines aspects of the current educational structure that has the capability to directly alter, negatively or positively, the lives of individuals.

*It's not because you're Black: Addressing Issues of Racism and Underrepresentation of African Americans in Academia* takes a bold look at how identity, stereotypes, and lack of resources affect what happens in colleges and universities. Also, it addresses the preparation of teacher interns in colleges and universities. Whether intentional or embedded in the minds of those in American culture, the results of Black underrepresentation in educational settings often carry devastating impacts on African American learners in diverse educational settings as well as career choices and opportunities for minorities who need them most. An increase in African American professors would, not only add diversity on college campuses but also, bring a unique perspective to the academy; a situation that would be beneficial to all. Using current facts, statistical analyses, and personal narratives, the authors present a compelling account of tradition and needed change in the American education system.

# Introduction

"In every crisis there is a message. Crises are nature's way of forcing change — breaking down old structures, shaking loose negative habits so that something new and better can take their place."
— Susan L. Taylor

Compared to past struggles of African Americans, the underrepresentation of Blacks in academia alone is not a matter of life or death. But as we look at the educational, psychological, sociological, and emotional implications of it, the effects are worth noting and are linked in a specific way that affects individuals' livelihood, health, and well-being, so as Einstein said, "It's all relative." Oftentimes, we hear, "it's not because you're Black" that the African American individual didn't get that job, loan, house, or taken seriously, etc. Many times, my White friends tell me that the unnecessary obstacles that I am facing are not because of my color, even though they don't know what I am going through nor can they possibly experience the challenges I face as an African American female; their Whiteness is not an issue here and is seldom thought of; there are countless examples and scientific research citing discrimination based on race today in the 21st century. Throughout history, in the midst of intense racial discrimination, a large percentage of American Whites have denied the existence of discrimination against African Americans. Even in the midst of blatant racial discrimination, before and during the Civil Rights Movement, numerous Americans denied that Blacks were treated unfairly.

Sometimes in higher education, African Americans cannot put their fingers on it, but they know something is not right when considering the following: fewer African Americans are considered for tenure-track positions, they are asked and, in some cases, expected to serve on several committees which limits their time to do research, and fewer Blacks work at prestigious institutions. Additionally, fewer Blacks are in charge of hiring or writing job descriptions.

In higher education, we need to have a serious conversation about why, in the second decade of the 21st century, there are so few African Americans holding faculty positions in higher education. Unlike some unsubstantiated conclusions that there are few accessible and/or qualified African Americans, individuals are available; it is the system of exclusion that has been one of the biggest culprit. The data are undeniable, and the impact long-lasting. But not to despair, there are organizations taking the lead in recruiting and supporting African American graduate students. These organizations provide a foundation and a system of networks for scholars of color, which often provides the support that they would not have otherwise.

This book takes a realistic look at the effects of underrepresentation of African Americans in colleges and universities. It highlights local, state, and national consequences facing America's educational future as the country becomes more diverse. It also looks at the challenges that Blacks face trying to get into the academy and issues that confront those once they are in the profession.

*Chapter One*

# African Americans and the Academy

## The Numbers

African Americans make up about 12% of the U.S. population, but in colleges and universities, Blacks make up an estimated 5.3% of the professoriate, a slight increase from 4% thirty years ago. And at higher ranking institutions, the number is significantly lower. A closer look reveals that more African Americans in the professoriate end up in non-tenure, administrative, or adjunct positions. In predominately White institutions, many Blacks report having little professional support and /or networking opportunities with colleagues within their programs. Traditionally when Blacks land tenure positions, the expected teaching and service workloads are higher than that of the Whites. The result is usually less time for conducting research and establishing a robust research agenda and publications. Research and publications are essential for achieving tenure. According to the Chronicle of Higher Education, in 2009 only 3.5% of African Americans were employed as full-time professors at American colleges and universities; the largest number of African American faculty were employed as instructors, 7.7%; assistant professors made up 6.6% of African American faculty; 5.6 % were employed as associate professors and 5.6% as lecturers. African American females hired in these positions outnumbered their male counterparts. A breakdown of the Chronicle's findings can be seen on Table 1.1.

Table 1.1. Percentages of Faculty Members,      Fall 2009

| | Total, race known | American Indian | Asian | Black | Hispanic | White |
|---|---|---|---|---|---|---|
| Professor | | | | | | |
| All | 175,658 | 0.3% | 7.6% | 3.5% | 2.7% | 85.1% |
| Men | 126,526 | 0.3% | 8.4% | 3.0% | 2.5% | 84.8% |
| Women | 49,132 | 0.4% | 5.3% | 4.7% | 3.0% | 86.0% |
| Associate | | | | | | |
| All | 146,594 | 0.4% | 8.6% | 5.6% | 3.7% | 80.0% |
| Men | 86,468 | 0.4% | 9.6% | 4.8% | 3.6% | 79.5% |
| Women | 60,126 | 0.5% | 7.1% | 6.6% | 3.8% | 80.7% |
| Assistant professor | | | | | | |
| All | 167,022 | 0.4% | 11.2% | 6.6% | 4.1% | 70.6% |
| Men | 86,188 | 0.4% | 12.4% | 5.3% | 4.0% | 69.2% |
| Women | 80,834 | 0.5% | 10.0% | 7.9% | 4.2% | 72.1% |
| Instructor | | | | | | |
| All | 101,125 | 1.0% | 5.5% | 7.7% | 6.5% | 77.5% |
| Men | 45,179 | 1.1% | 5.7% | 6.4% | 6.8% | 77.8% |
| Women | 55,946 | 0.9% | 5.4% | 8.8% | 6.3% | 77.2% |
| Lecturer | | | | | | |
| All | 32,450 | 0.4% | 7.1% | 5.6% | 4.9% | 76.7% |
| Men | 15,258 | 0.4% | 7.1% | 5.4% | 4.3% | 76.7% |
| Women | 17,192 | 0.4% | 7.2% | 5.8% | 5.4% | 76.7% |

Source: The Chronicle of Higher Education

So how do we interpret the implications of these numbers? First, we must acknowledge the likelihood of increasing the number of African American faculty. The good news is that the number of doctorates awarded to African Americans (U.S. citizens or permanent residents) continues to increase, although in small numbers. According to the

National Science Foundation, the number of doctoral degrees awarded to African American increased to a single year high in 2009. The number of degrees awarded in 2009 was 2,221 compared to 2,017 in 2008 and 1,799 in 2005. See Figure 1.1.

Second, a large majority of the degrees awarded to African Americans were in education. Overall, however, there remains a shortage of African American teachers in k-12 classrooms as well as in higher education. According to a 2011 report by the National Center for Education Information, African American teachers made up 7% of American teachers in k-12 public schools (Feistritzer, 2011). The percentage of White students in public schools decreased from 68% to 55% between 1989 and 2009. In 12 states, Whites made up less than 50% of student enrollment with African American students having the largest enrollment in Mississippi and the District of Columbia (U.S. Department of Education, 2011). The significance of these trends is the process of funding distribution in public schools in America. The schools in the poorest districts tend to get less funding and resources than schools in more affluent districts and are expected to improve academic achievement under these unequal circumstances. Usually, African American students are typically found in the poorest schools.

While African Americans received 6.9% of the degrees awarded in 2009, 14.5% of them were education degrees; among them 18.4% administrative, 17.2% teacher education, and 12.4 education research. Degrees in the social sciences made up the second largest area of awarded degrees to African Americans in 2009. The numbers of African Americans being hired in tenure positions lags behind the number of Blacks earning PhD's. These numbers question the excuse that there are not enough qualified African Americans to hire.

Figure 1.1

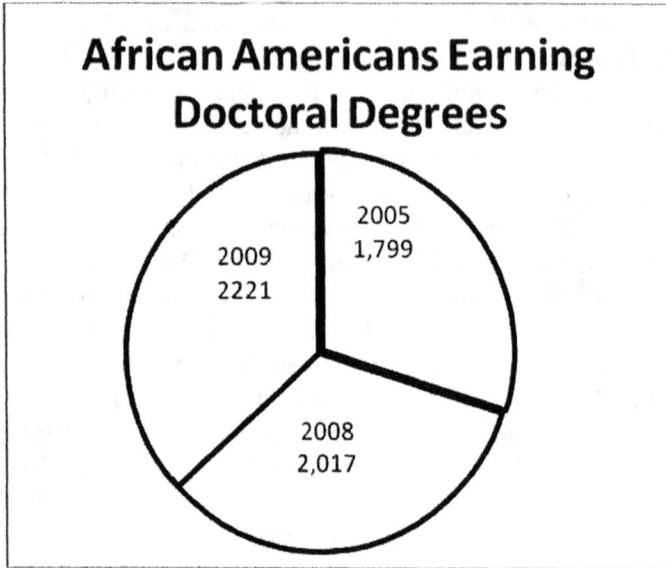

**African Americans Earning Doctoral Degrees**

2009 2221

2005 1,799

2008 2,017

Source: NSF/NIH/USED/USDA/NEH/NASA, 2009 Survey of Earned Doctorates

Third, we need to demand diversity in faculty hires. Numerous educational institutions list diversity as part of their mission statement and/or strategic plan, and for many it goes no further than the websites and brochures on which it is written even though racial and ethnic diversity tend to have positive effects on the education achievement and experiences of students. There could indeed be social factors that exist in academia that resists the notion to increase faculty diversity at colleges and universities. While some of the social forces may be inadvertent, there are others that are more purposeful. Numerous institutions of higher learning receive both state and federal funding- taxpayers money, and yet colleges and universities seem to be able to downplay or downright disregard the need for adequate minority faculty recruitment. The recent trend in America to end affirmative action has added another obstacle to hiring Black faculty. After the Civil Rights Law passed, numerous colleges and universities in America were cited for discriminatory practices that excluded or limited access to employment and education in institutions of higher education. The cited institutions were required to design a plan of action to eliminate the lack of access for minorities and were monitored by the Office for Civil Rights at the U.S. Department of Education and U.S. Justice Department. Many of the plans were ineffective. In many cases once the colleges and universities were no longer closely monitored, issues of civil rights were no longer a priority. Reverse discrimination claims filed by Whites added to the complexity.

Moreover, the idea of insisting on equity in hiring practices does not set well with some university leaders. Academia is frequently seen as a place for enlightenment and discovery and to some the thought of mandating diversity does not seem necessary. Recently, a somewhat disturbing trend of replacing race as diversity seems to be emerging. Some universities have *flipped the script* to limit their definition of diversity to lessen the importance of including African Americans in that definition and making the inclusion of other minorities, those that are usually well-represented, a more targeted goal. Still, increasingly race is being excluded from the definition of diversity and being replaced with other characteristics, such as gender, socio-economic status, or physical challenges. Indeed, diversity includes gender, socio-economic status, individuals with physical challenges, but it also includes race and ethnic backgrounds.

Sometimes there are perceived ideas that African Americans are incompetent in various professions, and that assumption tends to be similarly held in academia. Preconceived ideas of racial incompetence can be seen not only in interactions with colleagues, but also in the reactions of some students to African American faculty. Oftentimes, African American faculty experiences less job satisfaction than their White colleagues which tend to include feelings of isolation and alienation. Lack of mentoring and effective recruiting efforts are often cited as part of the problem. African American professors would, not only add diversity on college campuses but also, bring a unique perspective to the academy; a situation that would be beneficial to all. In a time of much needed education reform, utilizing effective resources should be a given, and employing a diverse faculty, including racial minorities, should be a major part of the process.

In the 1960's, Civil Rights laws and policies prohibited discrimination on the basis of race, color or national origin. A goal of the movement was to provide access to education and employment to minorities, and this included higher education. Among other things, Civil Rights laws established legal avenues for individuals and groups to file discrimination complaints against colleges and universities. Some may argue that despite the successes, the laws in many cases have not been properly interpreted or implemented to make substantial gains in the hiring of African American faculty in higher education. The higher education environment is often seen as a place of inclusion, insight, and intellect. However, the gains in employment opportunities for African Americans made in other professions are not represented in higher education.

## Defining Intelligence and Its Impact

Human fascination with issues of teaching and learning is documented as far back as Plato, who examined heredity versus experience. Plato surmised that knowledge, which is innate, when gained through psychic activity is stable and knowledge derived from the senses is unstable and not dependable. Since the time of Greek philosophers, issues of human development, in terms of individual versus group differences, and cognition and instruction have dominated the field of educational psychology; and yet, there is still much to examine, analyze, and explain.

Early studies in human development dealt with biological determinism that argued that development was based on genetic codes, which individuals could not radically alter. Sigmund Freud, a biological determinist, believed that developmental changes are neurologically and physiologically based and that a person's brain or physical functioning determines one's mental well-being. Other scientists like John Watson, the father of behaviorism, focused on the power of nurture in development. Watson believed that developmental outcomes could be orchestrated through environmental shaping. It was Jean Piaget, who more than anyone else, altered the course of human developmental research by his belief that both nature and nurture are involved in development.

Over the years the perceptions of intelligence have become more of a discussion about the environment and heredity— rather than past discussions focusing on heredity. We now can say without hesitation that our brains change due to environmental factors. Actively learning a different language or learning music can improve the brain processes. Both provide specific activities that can result in physical changes in the brain, including improved attention span and memory, and enhanced sequencing and structural processes. Other activities that show promise for brain function improvements are some video and board games, puzzles, the arts, and physical activities. Likewise, proper nutrition affects brain development and improvement. So what does it all mean?

Thus, learning is not determined only by heredity nor is it dictated by life experiences. Intelligence was thought of as a storehouse of information; more recently, intelligence is thought of as a series of interconnected knowledge structures. Ironically, past notions of intelligence are still impacting racial inclusion in numerous institutions and organization, including higher education.

While throughout the decades, the number of African American faculty has increased by a percentage or two, it represents an unanswered call for increasing the number of African Americans in academia. There are numerous thoughts about the cause of this underrepresentation, including the lack of Black candidates often cited by administrative leaders and, discriminatory practices, frequently cited by African —American PhD's.

To understand the low numbers of African Americans in the academy, one need to look no further than the history of how intelligence has been defined, studied, and researched. In the 1800's and the early 1900's anthropologists and psychologists agreed that Blacks had an inability to think abstractly and were the lowest dimension of mankind. Further, they claimed that the mental abilities of Blacks as compared to Whites were inferior, innate, and inherited (Ferguson, 1916; Garrett, 1963). Many of the researchers, scientists and psychologists harboring such beliefs were presidents, past presidents or members of the American Psychological Association, a respected scientific organization made up of psychologists and other scientists. So, researchers collected data with preconceived racial biases with the goal of substantiating the intellectual inferiority of Blacks. Basically, the research was the results of highly respected men in the field who believed that Blacks could not be very intellectual.

Higher education is all about intellectual ability— perceived or actualized. So claims by *experts* that Blacks are genetically inferior do not help facilitate recruitment efforts of African American faculty and can even trigger in some African Americans what social psychologist Claude Steele termed stereotype threat (1995), which suggests that while racism exists, stereotype threat is a more pervasive barrier to a truly integrated society in which individuals feel comfortable in mixed settings.

Every few years some research surfaces, making claims that Whites are genetically superior to Blacks or that Whites simply have bigger brains. Herrnstein and Murray (1994) made similar claims in their book the Bell Curve. One must also look at organizations and individuals who fund research projects focusing on ideas of Black inferiority. No matter how flawed the research, once the ideas are made public, there is relatively little focus on the errors and counterpoints made by the mainstream media. And so the image remains. It is similar to Wall Street speculators saying that gas prices will continue to rise, and then they do-not because of supply and demand or the cost of a barrel of oil but because powerful people said it, and thus it becomes so. In the case of race, a group hears negative stereotypes for so long that it hinders their ability to overcome the stereotype Steele's idea stereotype threat. Similarly, other groups hear the negative stereotypes of African Americans and perceive them to be totally true.

During the summer of 2007, I participated in an academic institute designed for doctoral students of color. For the first time in my academic career, I felt privileged to network and interact with other African American scholars, both male and female, who identified with the specific and unique challenges and obstacles I was experiencing on my doctoral path. I felt encouraged and empowered with an elevated sense of pride; there is a lot to be said for experiencing a sense of belonging and acceptance. And I imagined what it would be like to experience similar feelings as I attended a predominately White university in a doctoral program with only a few African American students and even fewer Black faculty members. The university I attended permitted me financial opportunities during my doctoral studies with assistantships and scholarships. And I discovered that numerous graduate students, as myself, were receiving financial support to obtain PhD's, and the majority was White. Almost half of doctoral students are awarded financial incentives such as assistantships, scholarships, etc. It is common for doctoral students to receive partial or full tuition for their studies and work as research and graduate assistants. Dissertations, by and large, are completed primarily because of persistency, and are not limited to denotative and/or connotative views of intelligence. I write that to say that sometimes there is a tendency for some minorities to feel guilty when they benefit from affirmative action or other programs when the majority tends to benefit by simply being born as a member of the majority in a country where Whites, in early American history, routinely received government subsidies in the form of land, benefits of the best neighborhoods, lower interest rates on homes and cars, etc. more means to affordable health care, and the opportunity to take advantage of the best education. Those advantages were passed down to their children, who were able to get a head start toward success.

## *Continuing the Fight*

There are aspects of the journey most students wish they had known prior to and during the pursuit of a doctoral degree. Earning a doctorate sometimes appears to be a maze of never-ending obstacles lined with secrets known only to the lucky few. Sometimes for African Americans students, the journey appears even more isolated and mysterious. The dissertation process will be addressed more in Chapter 4.

We live in challenging times of unrest with the first African American president in the White House in America. In an environment of resurfacing hostilities and the growth and attention of the Tea Party since the election of a Black president, negative stereotypes could possibly have a greater impact on not only the overall societal image of African Americans but also on racial identity development. The reaction to Barack Obama becoming President is an example of this notion of "it's not because you're black." The President has been called "a tar baby," "a liar," "a monkey," "unchristian," "a racist," "a socialist," "a dick," "not American," "a racist with a deep seated hatred for Whites." And it goes on and on. Although former President George W. Bush received some harsh criticism it was not aimed at his race, birth, patriotism, or Christianity; they were never questioned. As a country, we need to discuss issues of race and why these individuals feel so uncomfortable with Obama. These times have a tremendous effect on lives, physical and mental health, financial status, and future of individuals who are interconnected in numerous ways in our society.

Once in America, education held great promise for those who worked hard to achieve academic success–even the poor could improve their financial level. Many of us used the education ladder to climb out of poverty. But even in the 21$^{st}$ century, many opportunities are denied to African Americans–like decisions to ignore the recruitment and retention of African American faculty in institutions of higher education.

It is true that conditions have improved tremendously in education for African Americans, but there is still an enormous achievement gap between racial and socio-economic groups in America. In July 2011, the Pew Foundation released a report on the decline of wealth in America between 2005 and 2009, caused by the financial crisis with mortgages and the stock market in 2008. The report shows that Hispanic families suffered a 66% decline; African American families saw a 53% decline and Caucasians a 16% decline. While Hispanics saw the biggest the decline, African Americans were reported to have the lowest financial wealth at only $5, 677; Hispanics slightly higher at $6,325 but the most shocking aspect of the report is that the estimated wealth of Whites is $113,149.

Furthermore, the debate over affirmative action and negative views of colleges including race as a factor for enrollment and scholarships has added to more families taking out college loans. If we consider the fact that some institutions use children of alumni as criteria for enrollment, it is important to look at the history of who has been allowed to attend colleges over time; and yet, this does not receive much discussion when debating affirmative action. And if a student, through affirmative action, receives an opportunity, why is it only that opportunity that denied a White student? What about the thousands of non-minority students who were able to get into college because of other exclusive opportunities? And what about financing college? According to the U.S. Department of Education, between 1996-2011 student loan debt has more than doubled with an average debt now $25,000. How does a group survive with such disproportionate levels of wealth and education? It is through resilience and a healthy sense of identity.

Years of discriminatory practices in education and hiring, injustice and equality have resulted in a lack of African American faculty in colleges and universities in the U.S. The number of qualified candidates is improving as seen in the increase in black PhD's. But effective efforts to recruit and retain African American faculty are not improving. The "good ole boy" system is ignoring numerous qualified individuals and hindering their pursuit of successful careers.

*Chapter Two*

# Cultural Survival: A Matter of Resilience

## Racial Identity

The 2008 presidential campaign once again highlighted notions that White Americans are seen as more American than Blacks. A White man declared that he was voting for McCain and not Obama because McCain is a *full-blooded* American. African Americans tend to be considered less American and patriotic than Whites. Being American is often associated with being White. Sometimes groups moving here from other countries are seen as more American than African Americans, born here. Decade after decade something happens to try and reinforce the misguided idea that Whites are superior and Blacks are inferior. Developing a positive identity and sense of self is plagued with challenges for African American and yet despite that fact, numerous African Americans have managed to succeed in that same White/European society.

Although race relations in America are improving overall, racial discrimination is still very much prevalent in politics, the media, and numerous organizations and in higher education. Studies on how African Americans cope with and overcome discrimination have been conducted. And many findings have concluded that most successful Blacks have achieved success in the face of severe economic and social disadvantages and often with a strong, healthy sense of individual identity. Such individuals are resilient. Resilience is reflected in the individuals' well developed sense of self-esteem, willpower, optimism and a belief that they are in control of their lives despite differing opinions and the past of race relations and opportunities. Individuals who survive numerous obstacles and succeed usually come from environments where at least one parent or other adults have provided strong support, shown special interest, and held them to high moral and academic standards. In the

1960's and 70's during school integration, African American parents had to balance feelings of fear for their children going to an integrated school and breaking barriers to equal academic opportunities for them. There was a strong sense of community. Most of the adults felt responsible for keeping black children (not just their own) out of trouble, instilling strong moral values, and helping them succeed. When adults were around, children usually tried to keep out of trouble and do the right thing.

During the Civil Rights Movement, having pride in being Black was common. Symbols and slogans were frequently seen in magazines, on posters and T-shirts. Songs like James Brown's *Say it Loud, I'm Black and Proud* celebrated being Black in America in a time of great racial unrest and discrimination. There was a strong sense of racial identity and ethnic bonding.

Racial identity, which can be unique to each culture, plays a key role in individual development. Self-identity is basically how we understand who we are in our society. It is important to examine how individuals and groups construct an understanding of who they are and those things they deem important.

The environment plays a significant role in the forming of identity; it helps provide a testing ground whereby adolescents can question, interact, and form personal identities. Moreover, the environment consists of cultural norm, beliefs, and aspirations that allow young people to develop a sense of belonging and an understanding of where they are going. When young people have difficulty defining who they are and how they fit into their environment, problems can arise and lead to identity confusion or crisis.

The process of developing positive identities for Blacks, sometimes contradicts the society in which they live. It isn't always easy, especially for African American women, to believe that they are beautiful in a society where being skinny and White is portrayed as the model of beauty. From time to time, researchers in academia attempt to give credence to this portrayal. In May 2011, evolutionary psychologist Satoshi Kanazawa published an online article for Psychology Today entitled "Why Are Black Women Rated Less Physically Attractive than Other Women but Black Men Are Rated Better Looking than Other Men? Kanazawa wrote: even though objectively less attractive than other women, Black women (and men) subjectively consider themselves to be far more physically attractive than others." I had to laugh. His entire study was subjective with no objectivity anywhere to be seen! Kanazawa concluded: "It is interesting that Black women perceived themselves more attractive than other women." And why shouldn't they? This is an example of the self-confidence and self-worth these women had, despite the perceptions by others who disagreed. More reliable and relevant research would have examined the perceptions of attractiveness by these women in the face of societal images of beauty. Would so-called experts and publishers be as comfortable reporting bogus, racist research if more African Americans and other minorities were included in higher education as professors and researchers instead of serving mostly as adjunct instructors or lecturers? Most researchers objectively conduct studies on a daily basis. I do believe that African American researchers offer a different perspective to the field just in the way they ask questions, collect data, and interpret results.

For African Americans in a society with a devastating history of racial inequality, injustice, and discrimination, one cannot assume that African Americans cannot develop or have not developed a healthy sense of self. Similarly to other races, African Americans develop individual self-worth from interactions with family, friends, and others close to them.

My daughter's first negative encounter with her racial identity actually occurred when she was only three years old and attended, for the first time in her life, a racially mixed preschool. I picked her up from the school that day and instead of her usual jolly disposition, she had a solemn look on her face. "Mom, why am I bad?" she inquired. I was caught off guard a little.

"Erica, baby, you are not bad. Why do you think that?"

"Adam said that I am bad!" she exclaimed.

"Why would he say that?"

I remained calm. Adam's little face popped into my mind. I only knew a little about him; he was one of her White classmates, which didn't register in my mind until after Erica's next statement.

"His father said that all Black people are bad." As an African American parent, I knew that I would be having the *racial identity* conversation one day. I just never thought it would be at age three.

"Even at an early age, children are far from color-blind and by the age of three, many children already show bias across racial lines" (Civil Rights Coalition, 2002). How do individuals in minority groups develop a healthy self-identity in the midst of negative stereotypes often created by the majority group? The concept of racial identity is complex and hard to define. Even researchers have problems agreeing on its meaning and construction. They do, however, agree that the development of racial identity is significant in the overall make up of individuals and the ways in which people reflect and observe their environments (Tatum, 2003). Racial identity is often discussed in terms of biological features such as skin color. And yet racial identity involves so much more, including a social dimension.

Studies have been done on the development of racial and ethnic identity particularly for minority groups. However, the experiences of African Americans in the United States make the study of identity in African American culture different.

> Although many ethnic groups have experienced discrimination and oppression in the United State, the form of oppression that African Americans have faced is unique. While the worthiness of other ethnic groups has often been questioned upon their arrival in American society, no other groups' humanity was denied legally as property by the United States government for almost a century. (Sellers, Smith, Shelton, Rowley, & Chavous, 1998, p.18).

As a result, the concept of race traditionally has played a significant role in the lives of African Americans. For most African Americans, racial identity is manifested in very conscious ways. Russian psychologist Lev Vygotsky's theory of biological and individualistic reductionism contends that "whatever simple or complex psychological processes in question, the most interesting part or component of it, is not inherited biologically, but caused by and originated in a specific set of social interactions" (Kozulin, Boris, Ageyev, & Miller 2003, p. 434). Vygotsky believed that childhood development involves a series of contradictory changes which he termed critical periods. It is during these periods that a psychological structure of personality is formed. Regardless of the length of the critical periods, Vygotsky believed that children are affected in a fundamental way (1978). However, while others place race membership as the primary factor in shaping their self-concept and identity, some African Americans place little significance on race defining who they are. And still others try to change identities and incorporate characteristics of the White race. Numerous Black students have been told that they are "trying to be White" as they speak mainstream U.S. English and excel academically in educational settings. Decisions to earn good grades, speak mainstream U.S. English, or participate in majority dominated school activities have complicated the lives and identity development of many minority students.

Some African American students choose to balance their identity development with choosing to do things or participate in activities that the peers in their race shun. When these students choose to participate in majority activities, they are sometimes seen as deserting the race; much like individuals who move from family neighborhoods or towns to pursue their dreams are seen as deserting the family. This can sometimes lead to confusion for adolescent identity development. However, many Black students are committed to the values and behaviors of their African American peers and family members, and are able to develop ethnic pride and positive identity formation without denying themselves opportunities to participate in behaviors or actions they want to explore. Slowly, more minority students are ignoring imposed expectations based on race from both members of their racial group and from the majority group. But the academic achievement gap continues to widen between African American and Caucasians students. As an educator teaching and working with elementary and secondary students, I have been privileged to work with numerous talented, creative, and unique students. However, I have also seen the disappointment in their faces when others choose to limit them with lowered expectations based on stereotypes and ignore their future potential.

With the emergent of a more global society, numerous aspects of developments of identity will more than likely change. Some feel that African Americans have already lost a large portion of our cultural heritage because of the way they were said to have been brought into this country, and the consequent actions of society, lawmakers and leaders. Finding centuries of family ancestry is often a challenging task for African Americans. However, the last century provides a litany of careers and life successes by African Americans.

Identity development can influence whether or not an individual decides on a career in academia. It helps to determine individuals' beliefs about their ability to do a job— their self-efficacy. Researchers argue that regardless of an individual's level of talent and opportunity, self-efficacy beliefs provide a significant advantage to achieving success in numerous contexts, including school (Bandura, 1997; Maddux, 1995). Identity development is important for success. Work environments also impact what individuals believe about themselves and their abilities.

Having a history of inequality and discrimination can adversely impact the development of identity, especially for African Americans. So many times, African Americans are told that they are playing the *race card* or being paranoid when they mention racial inequality, injustice or discrimination. Sometimes discrimination is done in ways so subtle that the victims often wonder if they are imagining it. Story after story reveals examples of subtle uses of discrimination: rules suddenly changing once an African American is elected to office or obtains a new position on the job; denying African American doctoral students research opportunities with professors when their White counterparts are getting several opportunities; and African American students being disproportionately placed in special education program and underrepresented in gifted/talented programs. All of these cases have the potential of indirectly or directly impacting the financial livelihood and emotional wellbeing of the individuals. Low socio-economic status is disproportionately found in adults and youth of color, particularly African Americans.

According to the National Center for Education Statistics in 2007, 18% of children below the age of 18; 34% of those were African American as compared to 10% of White youth. With the recent economic crisis and large percentage of unemployed African Americans, the number of children in poverty is higher now. The parents of these students in elementary, middle, and high school are less likely to get involved in school activities, and the students feel less connected to school. African American children are more likely to attend schools with the least resources and employ the least qualified teachers. Furthermore, African American students, especially males are more likely to be suspended, expelled, or be referred to and/or placed in special education. Such conditions impose a wide range of stressors including issues of health, family instability and greater exposure to violence, and more limited extra-familial social support networks.

After repeated experiences of injustice, it is hard to get over it. And it can be equally as hard to trust others and believe that it won't happen again no matter how different the circumstance. Perceived discrimination has a significant mental effect on individuals.


*Psychology and Identity*

An emphasis on cultural and social influences on human development helped progress the direction of research. With the study of social influences on human development, Americans saw the beginning of educational changes in this country. As racial turmoil and social changes highlighted the 1950s, it was a psychologist and his wife studying African American children that helped alter the makeup of school systems throughout the country. Kenneth Clark and Mamie Clark (1950) launched the studies that became a key factor in the 1954 Supreme Court decision in Brown vs. the Board of Education of Topeka,

Kansas, that helped to initiate the end to racial segregation in public schools throughout America (Asher, 2003). The Clarks found that overwhelmingly African American children saw their skin color as ugly or even bad when compared to that of Whites. It was the argument that segregated schools only enhanced, if not perpetuated, this feeling of inferiority that was convincing in the Brown decision. The *color* studies used several techniques to investigate the development of racial identity and preference in African American children.

Much of the early psychological research in America on African Americans attempted to illustrate a widely held assumption that African Americans suffered from low self-esteem or self-hatred. This assumption was made without assessments to measure self- esteem in African Americans. It was assumed that since Blacks were devalued in American society that it would stand to reason that they suffered from low self-esteem and self-hatred. The research involved African American children and how they identified with Black and White stimuli such as dolls. It failed to measure self-esteem but measured aspects of the identity levels of the African American children. In addition, the results of this research were used to show how African American adults felt about themselves (Clark & Clark, 1950; Horowitz, 1936). There were some obvious problems with early racial identity research. First, it compared the responses of Black children to those of White; and White children's responses were seen as ideal. Researchers did not take into consideration the development of Black adults in terms of who they were as individuals and as members of a group. In the 1960's research designed to actually measure self-esteem showed results that revealed that self-esteem levels in African American children were often higher than those in Caucasian children (Marks, Settles, Cooke, Morgan, and Sellers, 2004).

Some ask why Blacks have strong beliefs about their abilities, given the lack of resources. African Americans have had to endure and "make do" for centuries. Many African Americans give the phrase "taking lemons and making lemonade" added meaning. But frequent discrimination or even perceived discrimination increases the psychological stress of African Americans. More research is needed to study the experiences of Blacks. For that to happen, an attitude of inclusion and a commitment to diversity are needed in higher educational institutions throughout America. It does not do anyone any good to pretend racism has just magically disappeared simply because we refuse to confront and combat it.

Minorities, especially African Americans, are often excluded from major research. True, there has been a lot of research conducted on

African Americans and racial identity. But researchers should include more African American students in studies, especially those involving cognitive development in young children. Some members of the psychology profession have not been too eager to embrace multiculturalism and thus have created cultural oppression. The book *Even the Rat Was White* argues that the field of psychology has been historically biased and ignored the contributions of psychologists of color (Gurthrie, 2004). A similar claim can be made about the history taught to students and the lack of research including African American students.   Effective and appropriate research should study cultural differences of emotional, physical, and cognitive development. While some researchers are hesitant about conducting research on minority students for fear of the results, to outright ignore this group is unprofessional as well as unethical. Oftentimes when African American faculty proposes research projects, they are asked if the project is race based as if such research is not important. African Americans want to do important research that is beneficial to all people and at the same time, there are aspects of the African American culture that are being ignored in the research.

Throughout my career, I have at times been the only African American in meetings and sometimes in the office; and more times than not, I have been expected to speak for or defend actions of other African Americans.   Thus, racial and ethnic identity becomes confusing and limited. To further complicate the situation for African Americans, early research on racial identity operated on misconceived assumptions. These assumptions were often based on researchers' biases.

With the increased opportunities for black scholars and more inclusive research, theories and racial identity models were designed. In 1971 psychologist William Cross developed theories of racial identity development published in his Nigrescence model that included a representation of the different stages individuals navigate in developing a Black identity. He revised the model in 1991 to include five stages. Cross provided an important foundation and he continues to revise the model.

The underground perspective as named by Gaines and Reed (1994) provided a different model to measure racial and ethnic identity. It focused on individuals' attitudes and beliefs about what it means to be black. This approach has roots that date back to W.E.B. Dubois. Dubois made known the struggle to be a Negro and an American simultaneously. He said that there is a natural conflict between America's negative view of the Negro and the Negro's own view of him or herself (Dubois, 1903).

Numerous Blacks realized this reality and began to look beyond White society's broader negative view and embrace their blackness.

As the research on racial and ethnic identity of African Americans continued and somewhat matured, the focus has been on using the self-concept of group identities to understand cognitive processes and structures (Phinney, 1992). This approach deals with the importance of race or ethnicity in the lives of individuals. More recently, researchers have made some progress in the study of racial and ethnic identity among African Americans. Sellers, Shelton, Rowley, and Chavous (1998) combined several existing theories to develop what they call the Multidimensional Model of Racial Identity (MMRI). This model strives to answer the following questions: How important is race in the individual's perception or self? And, what does it mean to be a member of this racial group? The MMRI has borrowed ideas from the mainstream perspective and merged them with the underground approach's emphasis on the qualitative meaning of being Black (Sellers et al., 1998). This model supposedly makes no value judgment on what represents a psychologically healthy versus unhealthy identity. There are three main assumptions in this model. First, it contends that identity, which is stable, can sometimes be influenced by situations. Second, social identities often vary in their significance to the individual. And third, the most valid indicator of racial identity is the individual's view of what it means to be black (Sellers, 1998). Some researchers have concluded that identity in African Americans is a lifelong, continuously changing process (Parham, 1989). Many times, racial identity seems to be a frame in which individuals categorize others (Chavez and Guido-DiBrito, 1999, p. 40). As Blacks are categorized and stereotyped as a group, maintaining a positive racial identity can be challenging, and psychological distress is increased.

Parham (1989) theorized that African Americans move through angry feelings against Whites to develop a positive frame of reference. And yet, whether or not racial identity is affected, African Americans are still enduring racial discrimination. Despite how African Americans try to hold onto positive racial identities, it appears that the results of many American policies and procedures are designed to overwhelmingly discriminate against African Americans in education, economics, health services, politics, and housing. For example, Sue (2003) writes that institutional racial oppression has created poverty rates for "African Americans that are three times that of Whites, provided health care that resulted in the highest infant mortality of any ethnic/racial group, and perpetuated living conditions that result in a life expectancy five to seven years shorter than Whites" (p. 52).    In addition, the Center for Community Change found that the practice of using income and credit history was seriously flawed. They found that a far greater number of Latino and African American home owners paid higher rates when their incomes rose! In other words, the lender's policy of using wage and credit history did not prevent disparities in lending rates (Sue, 2003). If conditions don't change will these realities of racism affect racial identities in African Americans?

Eighty percent or more African Americans report having experienced forms of racial discrimination whether subtle or blatant. We know that discrimination can lead to higher levels of psychological distress and lower levels of subjective well-being. This can result in anxiety or depression. Because there is no longer a strong organized focus on Black pride, individuals now need local support systems to help develop or maintain strong cultural awareness and pride. Racial discrimination undermines student academic achievement for ethnic groups, specifically African American students. Wong, Eccles, & Sameroff (2003) concluded that experiences of racial discrimination at school from one's teachers and peers predicts a decline in grades, academic ability self-concepts, academic task values, mental health (increases in depression and anger, decreases in depression and anger, decreases in self-esteem and psychological resiliency), and increases in the proportion of one's friends who are not interested in school and problem behaviors.

Eccles, Wong, and Peck (2006) also argue that anticipated future discrimination undermine African-American adolescents' academic motivation and performance. How prevalent is racial discrimination in the adolescent population?   Adolescents like adults reported racial hassles in their daily lives. Others perceiving them as a threat or incompetent were the most frequent occurrences of discrimination reported by adolescents. Being insulted or called a name or harassed was the least frequently reported occurrence.

Today, there are laws designed to end discriminatory practices; many say that affirmative action is no longer needed; and still others say that Blacks have the same opportunities as Whites in America. African Americans who buy into this idealistic and false reality of life for African Americans are left to question their identities as individuals as well as a member of their racial group.

What can parents, educators, and communities do to aid in the development of positive racial identities in all children and particularly the African American child? First, parents have to share information, including historical, with their children. Parents have to help children deal with the sometimes harsh realities of being a member of a minority group by being supportive and helping them discover the unique gifts the child has to offer. Second, educators have a unique opportunity as well as a responsibility to children, their parents, and the overall society to create classroom environments reflective of and appropriate to all the children they are teaching- and not just the ones who happen to be the same race or income level as the teacher. Teachers should strive to help children feel a part of the classroom environment (the norm) and not as if they are the other or abnormal race.

Relevant research contends that schools can either promote or undermine student developmental competence. One way to undermine it is to fail to provide differentiated instruction to all students, including those in low-achieving classes. It is undisputed that effective teaching affects adolescents' academic achievement. The student learning environment and quality teaching directly and indirectly affect student achievement. Classroom environments vary depending on the teacher as well as the student population which can be enhanced or hindered by teaching practices. A disturbing trend in numerous school systems is that the most needy, low achieving students often have the least effective teachers. Even though it may not be intentional, the consequences can be tremendous for these students. Too often in low-performing schools and in difficult-to-fill positions, teachers are hired without certification or hired to teach out their content area. Although teachers in these situations learn to survive, many times they use ineffective teaching strategies which often result in poor student achievement. Obviously, teachers can only do so much; students, parents, the community, and other stakeholders should do their part. But teachers do have an incredible opportunity to help or hinder students' ability to succeed or fail academically.

Third, communities should embrace all groups and include diversity in policy making for their towns and cities. Each group should have a voice in helping to create policy and improve living conditions for all citizens. If nothing else, the historical research on racial identity in African Americans has revealed the problems of oppression and how numerous African Americans have separated themselves from societal views to create their own image of what it means to be African American in a country that has traditionally devalued them, ignored their accomplishments, and treated them less than human.

*Social/Cultural*

   Racial identity while often discussed in terms of skin color, social and cultural issues significantly affect the formation of identify. The social dimension of identity includes how individuals interact with members of their racial group as well as well as with others. This socialization affects the mental well-being and in some cases the physical health of individuals. Social and emotional support can help buffer the effects of racial discrimination. Racial socialization is thought to help African Americans cope with discrimination and reinforce racial pride. It is also seen as effective in the development of identity. Racial socialization involves talks about cultural pride and the reality that people might teach African Americans differently because of skin color.
   Brown and Tylka (2010) conducted a study of young African American college students to examine the impact of racial socialization messages on the group's resilience and perceived discrimination. The study involved psychology students and students participating in multicultural organizations. Using different survey instruments, Brown and Tylka assessed racial discrimination, racial socialization, resilience, and social desirability. The researchers found that racial discrimination was negatively associated with resilience for students who received a greater number of racial socialization messages. They noted that the specificity and frequently of the messages had varying effects on the students. They suggested that messages supporting cultural awareness and understanding, preparation for coping with and negotiating discriminatory environments, and understanding the system of inequality are necessary for resilience, and thus success.
   Socialization can help offset the effects of negative stereotypes. Stereotypes have falsely portrayed African Americans and affected their employment and/or academic opportunities. "To stereotype is to assign identical characteristics to any person in a group, regardless of the actual variation among members of that group" (Aronson, 2004, p. 244). Aronson further states that stereotyping, although it may appear to be positive, is harmful to individuals. In America, African Americans have had to endure overwhelming negative images from all aspects of society, including the media, politics, and criminal justice. What does this do to racial and ethnic identity development? "If positive ethnic group messages and support are not apparent or available to counteract negative public messages, a particular individual is likely to feel shame or disconnection toward their own ethnic identity" (Chavez and Guido-DiBrito, 1999, p. 41).

As a child during the first year of school desegregation, I remember a White teacher discussing a geography lesson. The picture in our books showed a half-dressed Nigerian boy in his everyday environment. The child had my skin color and hair texture. As the other students, both Black and White, began to make fun of the boy's dark coloring, *nappy* hair, and his clothes, I was ashamed. I knew that I was an African descendant and that somehow I shared a biological bond to the child in the book. If the others made fun of him then I surely must exhibit those same embarrassing qualities and characteristics. The teacher did not discuss or explain but merely ordered silence throughout the room. Without further discussion, how then is a sensitive eight year old expected to handle this situation without a massive encounter with cognitive dissonance? Consequently in many cases, African Americans have been molded and forced to fit into the majority's view of what it means to be Black in American society.

Social experiences help provide individuals with a deeper understanding of mutual interchanges and ideological systems, emotional appropriateness, psychological process, and societal beliefs. During adolescence, social conditions can vary from individual to individual. However, adolescence consistently involves social expectations from parents, teachers, peers, and society. Numerous social variables affect adolescent development including one's ethnicity and family income. The family socioeconomic status affects adolescents in several ways including opportunity structure and parental values and aspirations. Social expectations of adolescents can differ from culture to culture and entail the rules, norms, and communication of the specific culture. Researchers found that dating, changing schools (from elementary to middle to high), and puberty are particularly stressful during adolescence. An integration of past identities, marked by childhood and one that replaces it experienced in society, is vital for continuation of identity achievement. The adolescent's trust of him/herself and those around him/her are important. This is a period when the adolescent must come to terms with herself as an individual and how she relates appropriately to society. The experience helps provide individuals with a deeper understanding of mutual interchanges and ideological systems, emotional appropriateness, psychological process, and societal beliefs. Essentially, identity allows the person a sense of continuity in social relationships.

Maintaining a cultural identity as an African American is often more elusive than developing an identity in a majority White/European society. African Americans probably more than any other ethnic group have had their history and cultural identity almost wiped out. As they have tried to establish a cultural identity, many of the new traditions have been seen as not real.

## Lingering Stereotypes

Just as many parents communicate different expectations for their male and female children, individuals knowingly or inadvertently communicate different expectations for people based on their race. Decades after integration, some schools continued to hold separate proms and other social activities for African Americans and Whites. In many cases, White parents did not want their children exposed to African Americans in a social situation like a prom. There was no doubt that lingering stereotypes of what would or might happen were the primary reason. Recent research on implicit bias provides significant findings on the pervasiveness of discrimination against African Americans. Implicit bias is defined as a social stereotype associated with attitudes and beliefs about a racial group and can influence future judgments and actions (Greenwald & Schwartz, 1998).

Throughout the decades, the media has been notorious for communicating acceptable careers and behaviors for African Americans and women. During my doctoral studies, one of my professors commented that stereotypes are good. It is common knowledge that stereotypes for African Americans tend to be more negative than for any other ethnic group. Even those starting out as a positive reflection of African Americans have a way of ending up having negative consequences. For example, the stereotype is that African Americans are good athletes seems fine on the surface; but the underlying message is that *jocks* are dumb and have an inability to be intellectual. How many coaches felt that African American males wouldn't make good quarterbacks because they didn't have the intellectual ability?

In recent years, negative stereotypes of African Americans are being made or insinuated more than ever before and in virtually all aspects of society. There is no hesitancy for those wanting to take this country back and restore it to the way it was during the days of our founding fathers. Blacks are told that we think about our past racial history too much, when it is the majority that wants to revel the past year after year—even the confederacy is hailed as a wonderful part of history that is worthy of continued celebration. Isn't it, or why isn't it obvious that this is offensive to many African Americans? It is perspective, and until we try to understand and value each other, tolerate our differences, and engage in a civil dialogue about race, nothing will change. The so-called Marriage Pledge drafted by an Iowa-based conservative group the Family initially stated that black children were better off during slavery than under the presidency of Obama. It stated:

Slavery had a disastrous impact on African-American families, yet sadly a child born into slavery in 1860 was more likely to be raised by his mother and father in a two-parent household than was an African-American baby born after the election of the USA's first African-American President. (2011)

After an outcry from the public, the group removed this section of the 2-page document. Why didn't the authors of this document realize the implication of that statement before publishing it? Additionally, Fox News has been notorious about heaping as many negative stereotypes as possible on Obama. Among them, they published an article entitled Obama's Hip-Hop BBQ Didn't Create Jobs after the celebration of Obama's 50th birthday. A diverse group attended the party not just hip hop mogul Jay-Z, but jazz and R&B musicians, entertainers, athletes, and lawmakers. But it was called a hip-hop BBQ because of the color of the President and the stereotypical image they want to portray of him; whether admitted or not, this is a strategic move in a country where Black stereotypes intimidate some individuals or diminish the authority of African Americans in prominent leadership positions. In the spring of 2011, Eric Bolling of Fox Business Network referred to the President's guests as hoods. And later Bolling commented, "where is our leader...entertaining rappers in the east room of our white house or chugging a few 40's in Ireland while tornadoes ravage Missouri."

Even in January 2012, candidates vying for the Republican nomination for president of the United States did not hesitate to stereotype African Americans as financially dependent on food stamps and void of work ethics and role models (except for the criminal elements). Campaigning in Iowa where the Whites makeup about 91% of the population, Rick Santorum said:

It just keeps expanding [social program]. I was in Indianola a few months ago and I was talking to someone who works in the department of public welfare here, and she told me that the state of Iowa is going to get fined if they don't sign up more people under the Medicaid program. They're just pushing harder and harder to get more and more of you dependent upon them so they can get your vote. That's what the bottom line is… I don't want to make black people's lives better by giving them somebody else's money; I want to give them the opportunity to go out and earn the money. [Applause]. And provide for themselves and their families. [More applause].

Such rhetoric continues the practice of stereotyping African Americans in a negative manner, and the applause and pure acceptance of these comments by the white audience are problematic in a society where discriminating against Blacks in housing, wages, etc. directly affects the health and livelihood of African Americans disproportionately when compared to Whites.

Speaking to senior citizens in New Hampshire, Newt Gingrich said:

Now there's no neighborhood I know of in America where, if you went around and asked people would you rather your children have food stamps or paychecks, you wouldn't have a majority saying they'd rather have paychecks…And so I'm prepared, if the NAACP invites me, I'll go to their convention to talk about why the African American community should demand pay checks and not be satisfied with food stamps. (2012)

Gingrich, along with other Republicans, characterized President Barack Obama as a food stamp president, leaving one to question- is it because he's black that he earned this distinction, or is it because the country has more cases of poverty due to the housing bubble and Wall Street crash, both of which were not caused by the first Black president?

Of course, these politicians were rebuked, but once again the damage had been done. Both claimed that the comments were not meant to be racist; Santorum even denied saying *Black people,* and instead said he uttered *blah people.* However, listening to the taped speech, it sounds like Black people to the majority of listeners. These unprovoked attacks on Blacks serve to scare Whites and energize the Republican base, but they also make it challenging for many African Americans to succeed in the midst of these negative comments and embedded stereotypes–issues that we are not comfortable discussing in our society.

My experience has been that it is easier for young people to discuss issues of differences, including race. When I was a doctoral student, I did a project with a group of high school students involving culturally-relevant issues. The group consisted of: 4 African American females, 2 Caucasian females, 1 Hispanic female, 1 African American male, 1

Caucasian male and 1 Egyptian male with a mean grade point average of 3.3. The students were shown a series of primary and secondary historical documents and voiced their thoughts in a "think aloud" format, where they said the first thing that came into their mind. Since they were not familiar and did not use this format often, they practiced the procedure prior to the activity.

Each student, one at a time, was given two sets of documents during two separate interviews over a two-week period. One set of documents included school desegregation at the University of Alabama and the infamous "stand in the schoolhouse door" by then governor, George Wallace. The documents presented differing perspectives of the issue. The written documents included: two personal accounts from two African American women, Autherine Lucy and Vivian Malone, who were instrumental in integrating the school; Wallace's 1963 inaugural speech, as he vowed "segregation now, segregation tomorrow and segregation forever"; a proclamation by Wallace that argued that school desegregation should be a state mandate and not the decision of the federal government; a newspaper account of President John F. Kennedy federalizing Alabama National Guard after Wallace turned back African American students seeking to enroll at the university; a historian's account summarizing the aftermath of the first African American student enrolled; an excerpt from a high school U.S. history book summarizing the 1963 events; and a telegram from President Lyndon Johnson asking a local newspaper publisher to support the enactment of the Civil Rights Bill.

There were also three photographs used. One photograph was a wide shot in front of the Foster Auditorium used to show the gathering of troops, guardsmen, and the media during Wallace's stand against desegregation. This photo shows dozens of Alabama troopers and newsmen in front of the building as then Alabama Governor George Wallace speaks to the U.S. marshals as they stopped the first attempt to register two African American students; state troopers are atop of the building. This photograph was selected to show students the conflicting events of the day as well as an example of the magnitude of activity going on at the University.

Another photograph was a close up of Governor Wallace with his state troopers blocking the door of Foster Auditorium to keep the African American students from enrolling. The photograph depicts Wallace's firm stand on the issue of state's rights. The last photograph is of Vivian Malone smiling as she is being escorted by federal marshals to a dormitory at the University of Alabama. This photograph was taken after

Malone successfully enrolled at the University despite the opposition. The group of students was effective at piecing together the historical events that occurred decades before they were born and a few miles from their current homes. Only one student had seen all three photographs. They had all seen the close up of Wallace blocking the entrance into the auditorium. And the only written account they were familiar with came from textbooks used in their classes. None of them had read the interviews of Malone and Lucy or the historian's account of the events. The students were empathetic as they verbalized their thoughts and opinions of these events. I was amazed at how easily they could express their beliefs about racial issues. Perhaps, it was because each student was one-on-one with a researcher.

A majority of the students selected the photograph of Vivian Malone smiling, as she is being escorted by federal marshals to a dormitory, as being the least accurate. Some commented that they thought Malone was just smiling for the cameras while inside she was afraid of being murdered. On the other hand, the students believed that the personal interview account of Autherine Lucy was the most trustworthy. During the debriefing phase, the group did not hesitate to discuss racial tensions. They understood Wallace's arguments about state's rights, and they thought it admirable that he eventually changed his opinions about school segregation of Blacks and Whites in Alabama. However, they didn't understand the reasons for wanting to separate people based on race. One student commented, "I guess people sometimes make mistakes, but he [Wallace] should have come to those conclusions when those kids were throwing bricks at Autherine Lucy."

Another student said, "I was thinking about when I went to Central High School in Arkansas, and I saw all of the statures and everything. And 'cause I can't imagine *like* somebody telling me that I can't do something *like* because I have blond hair. Overall, the students displayed a maturity in confronting issues that many adults are afraid to discuss.

Yes, we have racial stereotypes, and it is difficult to see passed them. They shouldn't limit us or put us in a box based on societal perceptions. At the end of the day, I will still disagree with my college advisor who said that stereotypes are good. While some people have benefited from them, overall, they are limiting and can be destructive to the development of identity development.

Higher education should be a place for insight, ideas, intellect, and tolerance —the ivory tower. It is interesting that faculty like children in a cafeteria tend to congregate in groups based on race. And when there are few African American full-time faculty, how do groups form?

Frequently, African American faculty is not included in the groups. Even when the institutions have a mentoring program in place, they are often ineffective and symbolic at best. Developing and negotiating strategies for dealing with alienating environments such as institutions of higher education are essential for minority faculty members and in particular African Americans.

*Chapter Three*

# Environment of Change

## Embracing Change

Fortunately, the news for African Americans in higher education is slowly improving. But thousands of individuals have been denied access and opportunity. One way some organizations have chosen to address this issue is through increased minority recruitment. There are several organizations actively recruiting and supporting minorities in the professoriate. The organizations are sometimes specific to career choices and/or subject specific. Others are more general and are highly competitive. So despite perceptions by some in society that unqualified African American scholars are given opportunities that Whites in similar situations would not have, are simply not true. First, most African Americans who qualify and compete for support from these organizations have usually overcome surmountable difficulties to be able to meet the often stringent requirements. Second, since African Americans were denied an education for centuries, many of the benefits and opportunities that Whites enjoyed in America have helped their generations of offspring to get a head start and/or significant financial and educational advantage. Therefore, it is fitting that recruiting African Americans into higher education should be a priority if not a debt owed

## *SREB*

The Southern Regional Education Board (SREB) is a nonprofit and nonpartisan organization started in 1948 and funded by governors and legislators. The organization works with state leaders, schools, and educators. SREB has several programs in place to help facilitate educational opportunities for underrepresented students in higher education. They have college and career readiness programs to help students who enroll in college graduate. One of its goals is to increase the number of minorities completing doctoral degrees in science, technology, engineering or math. Partnered with the NSF Alliance for Graduate Education and the Professoriate (AGEP), SREB provides support services to prepare its scholars for careers as college faculty members. SREB supports qualified candidates financially and also helps identify career opportunities. There are 16 member states and more than 300 scholars actively pursuing Ph.Ds. Of that number, the organization cites 80% that have begun academic careers in higher education. SREB collects and analyzes education data to improve services to their participants (Southern Regional Education Board, 2012).

## McNair

The McNair Scholars Program was established in honor of Robert E. McNair, an African American astronaut who died in 1986 when Space Shuttle Challenger exploded. McNair is a federal TRIO program funded at 194 institutes across the U.S. and Puerto Rico and designed to increase the number of graduate degrees awarded to students from underrepresented groups. The scholars are typically first-generation college students or members of underrepresented students in higher education (McNair Scholars Program, 2012).

## Holmes Partnership/AACTE

As cited in my 2009 dissertation, the Holmes Partnership was an organization that collaborated with colleges of education, K-12 schools, and communities to support teachers, provide resources, and network with and support minority graduate students. The organization grew out of the Holmes Group. In an effort to reform education through the use of professional development schools (PDSs), the Holmes Group proposed its vision to help build relationships between schools and teacher training institutions. In 1986, the Holmes Group set forth their vision of good teaching, recommending an agenda of actions in the publication *Tomorrow's Teachers* (1986). The Holmes Group later became the Holmes Partnership, symbolizing more inclusive membership and mission. Later, in another publication Tomorrow's Schools (1990), the group put forth its recommendation of what should be accomplished by PDSs, which consisted of six basic principles deemed as central. The principles were detailed as: (1) curriculum and instruction should allow all students to seriously participate in learning for understanding, resulting in learning for a lifetime; (2) PDSs should attempt to organize classrooms and schools as learning communities for the benefit of all students; (3) A commitment should be made so that teaching and learning is intended for everybody's children in an effort to overcome educational and social barriers; (4) All adults involved in the PDSs are expected to go on learning as well as the students; (5) There should be thoughtful long-term inquiry into teaching and learning, whereby the PDS faculty working as partners promotes reflection and research on practice as a central aspect of the relationship; and (6) The principles demand profound changes calling for the invention of a new institution as a different kind of organization structure, resulting in better preparation for school faculty (Holmes Group, 1990).

Estimates of the formalized school-university partnerships indicate that there are more than 600 operational in the United States (Reed, Kochan, Ross, & Kunckel, 2001). The PDS movement of the 1990s brought with it efforts to reform education by linking teachers and university faculty in collaborative partnerships (Mebane & Galassi, 2003; Teitel, 2001). The Holmes Group, a consortium of research universities later known as the Holmes Partnership, described the PDS as "designed to serve itself and professional education the way teaching hospitals serve medical education" (Holmes Group, 1986, p. 8).

Typically, PDSs are clinical field sites where school and university partners work collaboratively to reach common educational goals. The concept of the PDS was designed particularly to address teacher and teacher education problems. But a universal definition has not been agreed on because of the uniqueness of each individual program. Most PDSs are constantly evolving leaving little time to capture what they are doing (Teitel, 2001; Valli, Cooper, & Frankes, 1997). Usually with the establishment of a PDS partnership, schools are undergoing other changes related to state and/ or national educational reforms (Metcalf-Turner & Fischetti, 1996).

Despite the Holmes concept about PDSs, no official criteria are being used for justification and determination of whether or not a program should be deemed a PDS (Reed, Kochan, Ross, & Kunckel, 2001). Additionally, while the concept has had great appeal to teacher educators, pre-service teachers, and administrators, critics have raised serious questions as to its viability (Gardner & Libde, 1995). Most of the initial criticism focused on Holmes' comparison of teachers to medical doctors. Some argued that teaching cannot be professionalized to follow medicine's example because of its low level on the occupational hierarchy (Cornbleth, 1988; Cornbleth & Gottlieb, 1989). Other critics saw it as elitism for some teachers to be labeled professional and not others based on PDS participation and argued that the notion a school can become a learning community is naïve due to the established roles of PDS stakeholders (Judge, 1988; Barth, 1988).

Another important aspect of Holmes is the recruitment and retention of minority graduate students which started in 1991. In 2011, the American Association of Colleges for Teacher Education (AACTE) became the official home of the Holmes Scholars Program. The scholars program was designed to help minority doctoral students by enriching scholarly activities/experiences, provide mentorship and peer support, and offer professional development opportunities. Today, the Holmes Partnership has supported more than 600 underrepresented minority doctoral students. More than 200 of the students are employed in tenure-track positions at colleges and universities.

As a Holmes scholar, I had the opportunity to network with numerous minority graduates. The activities gave me a sense of belonging that allowed me to go back to my doctoral studies with a sense of confidence and hope. The Holmes alumni association provided mentors in academia or leadership positions who were always understanding and willing to help. Additionally, I had the opportunity to present my research at national conferences which I would not have had otherwise. During the conference presentations, others provided feedback to help me improve my research and writing. I attended two summer institutes where I met with leaders in organizations such as the American Research Institute and the National Center for Education Statistics, and politicians. Personally, the experience I had as a Holmes scholar helped me to see others like me and lessen the burden of being a minority during my doctoral studies.

## A Series of Networks

These and similar organizations are important in helping to lessen the underrepresentation of African Americans in academia. Without such organizations, some of the students say they would not have made it through their studies nor earned graduate degrees. There are now efforts by several organizations to mentor minority faculty early in their careers. The value of these organizations can never be fully realized in terms of the emotional, mental, and psychological benefits many of the participants have received. However, once the students have earned the degrees, the work environment presents new challenges. One of the biggest challenges is the lack of guidance about the academic workplace. Another one is not being considered for top jobs or tenure-track positions. It will take more than these organizations to significantly change the lack of diversity in academia. But at least, there are systematic efforts by organizations, though colleges and universities should take the lead in recruiting and retaining minority faculty.

*Chapter Four*

## Options for Blacks in Higher Education

### The Careers

There are numerous careers for doctoral graduates. In higher education, there are staff, faculty and administrative jobs. For African Americans, the careers in higher education are mostly at the staff and administrative levels. Even in the 21$^{st}$ century, it is difficult for minorities to, not only obtain tenure-track positions at colleges and universities, but once they get them, the tenure process often becomes a nightmare. This chapter discusses several career options and strategies that African Americans in higher education have chosen.

*The Post Doc*
*By Orville Blackman, Ph.D.*[1]

In this section, I will detail how the opportunity to pursue a Post-Doctoral Fellowship helped to salvage and reshape my research agenda. After many challenges due to the loss of committee persons over a two year period, my research agenda was almost nonexistent and I was destined for the job market without the tools I needed to become successful. Kudos should be given to my mentors who had only a year later agreed to lead my dissertation. They subsequently agreed to mentor me through a Post-Doctoral appointment.

So I was about to defend my dissertation and the reality of finding a job loomed large. With some naivety I had entered academia with the

---

[1] Orville Blackman, PhD, is the director of the graduate business programs at Indiana Wesleyan University in Marion. He has a doctorate from the University of Louisville in leadership and organizational development.

assumption that a Ph.D. will automatically pave a way for high paying prestigious job. It was not very long after I began my work on a Ph.D. student that I realized that I was trading a high paying job as a corporate consultant for the rights to become one of an elite group called "Doctor". It was not the prestige of earning the degree that was my motivation; however, it was a genuine desire to make a contribution to the advancement of the careers of many students who pursue education with the hope that they would acquire skills to be marketable and effective in their jobs.

Many assumptions about higher education were wrong. The reality is that regardless of extensive corporate and international experience, I was about to enter the world of academia as a novice. It became very clear that the academic culture had little room for experiences alone. Those experiences needed to be grounded in academic rigor and validated through the scrutiny of a panel of professors who served on my dissertation committee. To learn how to become a professor, I had to integrate my experiences to the learning that I was about to experience. I had to become a student in my chosen discipline, and that meant that I had to become accustomed to being led and fed rather than being the successful leader and advisor that I was in the corporate world.

Weeks after I arrived on campus, I sought to make connections with faculty members that could help me to shape my research agenda. My experiences as a corporate consultant influenced my decision to return to the university to pursue a doctorate. At the time I entered the doctoral program, I had every intention return to the corporate arena to practice my skills. Through my interactions with managers and front line workers in the corporations where I served as organizational development consultant, it was very evident that that there was a disconnect between higher education and the corporate world. Students were graduating from universities with credentials and skills that were not properly aligned with the work that the students wanted to pursue. Many students were graduating with liberal arts degrees and then seeking to find places in the labor market. Similarly, employers use credentials as the default for hiring people for different roles. Once a student had earned a degree, it almost guaranteed entre into the labor market. What I soon found was that organizations were spending millions of dollars retraining employees to develop employee skills to proficient and relevant levels.

Employers also admitted that many degree holders were placed in positions of influence because of a combination of credential and tenure not because of a skill set that was effectively matched with the job that the employee was expected to perform. I assumed that I could legitimately pursue a goal of becoming a "corporate doctor" but I soon found that was consistent with the university's goals. It became apparent that the university's mission was to train doctors to be academics who serve in higher education when I was soon shut out of a graduate assistantship because I had declared that I wanted to return to the corporate world and practice my trade with a greater understanding of how people should be academically prepared to be high performing employees.

Soon after I realized that I was not going to succeed with such a stated agenda, I capitulated and reframed my dialog to be consistent with the expectations of my supervising professor. However, I began to formulate a strategy to both thrive in the higher education arena and find a way to remain connected to the corporations I had previously served. There was no change in my conviction that the university had to do a better job of matching academic preparation with the skill needs of the labor market. Unfortunately, there were no scholars in my school who had done this type of research before, and so I had to select the person whose research was most closely aligned to the scholarship that I intended to pursue. Once I had navigated the initial errors I thought I could get myself on track to establishing a research agenda that would empower me to be a highly skilled academic who could maintain relevance to the labor market.

The enthusiasm with which I entered the doctoral program never waned despite having to navigate the early challenges. I recall Goffman's (1959) work where the author opined that we are all actors on stage, presenting a façade that we want others to believe is the true representation of self. We become who we need to become for the purpose of presenting the best face to the audiences to whom we are playing. Paralleling the Ph.D. application process, admission to the program, and schooling experience with Goffman's analogy with the theater–I auditioned–the application process, was casted–admitted to the program, and became an actor in a play that at sometimes felt like comedy, oftentimes–a drama, but at other times had the characteristics of a tragedy.

At the time of matriculation, I was one of 20 students in a cohort who entered the university at the same time. Our experiences were destined to be different–in some scenes of the *Ph.D. play,* people were happy and seemed to be doing well–the comedy. In other scenes, international students who were limited by the time permitted by their governments were resolute and purposeful–the drama. Yet in other scenes, others experienced horror with trying to complete their degrees–

the tragedy. While we were all casted for the same play, we needed to learn the roles that we were expected to play and how to perform on the university stage if we were going to successfully navigate the politics of higher education.

Goffman's (1959) work became more poignant as I observed the inner workings of the university. Undergraduate and master's students in the school seemed oblivious to the fact that they were seeing only what the university *actors* wanted them to see. On the other hand, since doctoral students had to be mentored by faculty, and often performed roles as teaching and graduate assistants, we did not only see the *front stage* we saw the *back stage*. The *back stage* exemplified the challenges that doctoral students from my cohort students were about to face. Conflict between administration and the faculty had reached a level that the very mentors on whom doctoral students depended, were leaving the university at a steady rate. By this time I lost the one professor who could help me create a research agenda that aligned higher education with the needs of the labor market.

I subsequently lost three more mentors in the cleansing process that the college experienced. One by one they left as I adjusted my research agenda to match the next assigned professor. By the time the time the fourth professor left, my research agenda had lost its identity and I had lost my real purpose for returning to the academy. I soon found that my scene in the play had changed from the early enjoyment of a comedy to the fear and horror of a tragedy. No one was left that could help me salvage 82 pages of a dissertation and two and a half years of doctoral study. My doctoral program was designed to be a logical process that prepared me for success in academia but had become akin to a jigsaw puzzle with missing pieces. It appeared that the picture could never be completed and I was destined for failure. This was a genuine fear because we were told that the national statistic for failure to complete the Ph.D. program was about 50 percent. Was I destined to become a negative statistic?

Admittedly, I was not the only one of my cohorts to be in such a difficult position. More than two-thirds of my cohort class were in the same position and were desperate for answers that the university could not provide. I was intent that I would not become one of the casualties. I needed to make a decision about moving forward. I thought there must be someone here at the university who could help me salvage my education. My research agenda was now non-existent and I was less than a year away from entering the job market without a clear agenda, very few publications or presentations and certainly not in a position to compete for scarce jobs in the best universities.

I had less than a year before my funding ran out. I had managed to secure a graduate assistantship that was more aligned with my experience in service learning than in my initial research interest. I believe that God had provided this unusual opportunity for me and I made the best use of the opportunity. I participated in many activities that were not directly related to my research agenda, but I was able to integrate the learning and experience from that graduate assistantship with my course of study to enrich my overall doctoral preparation.

Remaining encouraged throughout the process was not easy. However, I had come to the university and found other colleagues who had already invested as many as five years and were still not yet writing dissertations. In an unorthodox way I felt that if others had been in their programs for such a long time and survived, I could survive the telling blow of a botched dissertation and a dismantled committee to help me through.

Then came the new day! Like David the son of Jesse, I arose with a great sense of purpose and with confidence that I could slay the giants that confronted me. "Today is the day that I will find a new dissertation chair," I said to myself. So I left the house and went to the college and approached the newest senior faculty member who was employed by the college. I figured that since he had arrived less than six months previously, with a large federal grant, he was unlikely to leave the university before I completed my degree. He also had an established research agenda with scores of publications and presentations. He would become an ideal mentor. I thought that he could help me salvage my dissertation, but I went to his office unannounced knowing that he may have required me to start my dissertation all over again.

I had purposed that I was not going to dredge up the history of education misfortunes; I was not going to blame anyone for my demise. This new mentor and coach were to believe that I had now reached this point for the first time so that there would be no perception that I was bringing unwanted baggage to the discussion. As I walked through my new mentor's office door he welcomed me in to sit. I asked for 10 minutes and he gave me 90 minutes of his time. This was a good sign that I was about to see the revival of my dissertation.

To salvage the work that I had already completed, I introduced my original dissertation idea to my new mentor with the hope that I would not have to discard the work I had already completed. He found no kinship with the original study idea, so I finally accepted that I would have to rewrite my dissertation completely. It was evident that the hours of research and the 82 pages I had completed were now history. I remember leaving his office that day with mixed emotions. I was happy that he had agreed to mentor me, but sad that I had to start over. On the positive side, I left with new ideas, and resources that could help me salvage my education.

In less than a year, and with expert guidance, I completed a dissertation. I worked tirelessly–every day of the week for several hours each day. Completion was like an obsession. I could not afford to have another committee collapse before I completed my work. I was so driven that I did not tell my colleagues that I had decided to start all over again. It is only when I was near completion of the dissertation that I had the courage to tell them that I had to completely rewrite and research a new study. I had feared that if I had told too many people about my challenges, their concern for me would have negatively impacted my confidence and my willingness persist. I give kudos to my wife and daughter who were my comfort and encouragement during that very tough period of my doctoral studies.

The establishment of a new mentor-mentee relationship signaled the re-launch of my academic career. Through this new relationship, I completed my dissertation, met other scholars who were instrumental in shaping my research agenda and was afforded the opportunity to work with my mentor as a Post-Doctoral Associate. The role of Post-Doc was not only a desirable one, but it was necessary because I had not been adequately prepared to compete for a job in the nation's best universities, nor was I adequately prepared to thrive and become eligible for tenure in the three years that I would have been required to demonstrate competence.

By the time I had completed my dissertation I was mentally ready to return to the corporate world but my mentor made the offer to retain me as a Post-Doctoral Associate and this negated the need to leave the academy immediately. As a new Doctor in the academy, my mentor thought that I had begun some important work and suggested that I remain at the university to become a more established scholar. At a time when thousands of Ph.D.'s were graduating but not finding the jobs they wanted, this was an attractive offer. Some of my colleagues suggested that the role of Post-Doc was nothing more than a glorified Graduate Assistant and that I would waste another two years that could have been dedicated to building my own scholarship agenda. This could not be further from the truth. The Post-Doc became my ticket to success. It rejuvenated my academic career, offered me opportunities that I could not have developed on my own and allowed me to develop my agenda in a supervised environment.

As a Post-Doctoral Associate I was afforded the opportunity to be mentored by two nationally recognized scholars; participate in the writing and presentation of scholarly briefs for the department of Education in Washington, DC, represent the University at several conferences and colloquia, present papers at national conferences and refine my research agenda. I am confident that the success I now enjoy now as a scholar was built on a foundation that was introduced through the writing and defense of my dissertation, but established through the post-doctoral experience.

The Post-Doc is distinguished from the role of graduate assistant through the establishment of one's own research agenda, but under the guidance of a mentor. The Post-Doctoral scholar is respected as a junior colleague, invited to participate in scholarly activities and discussions, and participates in planning meetings that allows him or her to observe the back stage workings of higher education.

## Establishing a Research Agenda

At the time one enters a doctoral program, the student should have an idea of what he or she proposes as a research agenda. Needless to say, with very little understanding of what the doctoral program experience would be, the ideas that the student has on entering the program will be modified as the student gains academic knowledge and experience. In my case, my research agenda changed many times during the course of my study becoming more refined each time. However, some of those changes were catalyzed by the changes in academic supervisors.

I wrote earlier in this chapter that my research agenda was compromised by the constant departure of my assigned mentors. However, my primary interest in workforce development never changed. The Post-Doctoral fellowship provided a great opportunity for the establishment of that research agenda–without which I would have earned a degree but not develop the competencies that would help me become established as a researcher. In my current role as Director of Graduate Business Programs, my previous research and training are directly impacting my ability to (a) lead and motivate an academic team, (b) engage staff and faculty in creating a vision for our Graduate Business Division, (c) implement a research based model of curriculum development that aligns higher education to the labor market and (d) design and implement the methodology to create rigorous and relevant business programs.

So what is a research agenda? A research agenda is defined as a plan and focus on issues and ideas in a subset of a field of study (Reedy & Murty, 2012). Immediately upon being offered the Post-Doc position, I gained access to several resources including scholarly articles, books, and data that were relevant to my research interests. More importantly, I had direct access to senior scholars who helped to shape many of my rough ideas into meaningful topics and research projects. They also gave feedback on the best statistical methods for data analysis. My learning experience escalated at a rate that could not be achieved in my doctoral program. Statistical methods to which I was introduced in classes using small sample sizes were applied to large scale projects some of which were commissioned by the United States Department of Education. In addition to my research skills being enhanced, my writing and presentation skills were developed. Sitting across from me in another office was the editor of an academic journal who vetted my work and made suggestions about how I could improve my reports.

Because my research interests closely matched the research center where I acquired my Post-Doctoral fellowship, I was allowed to concentrate my efforts in the areas of my interest. I spent much time researching college program development, college student interests and engagement and labor market trends and skill requirements. This work was an expansion of my dissertation and I built on the research that was done in my doctoral studies. It is now three years since I completed my fellowship and my expertise in this subject area is highly valued in my current work. By actively engaging in research that informs policy, I am either collecting or supervising the collection of data that is used in decision making on a day to day basis. I am also fully engaged in training and developing members of the business team to do similar work.

A rewarding learning experience was having the opportunity to work directly alongside senior scholars. By engaging in their projects I acquired relevant research skills, and learned how to prepare reports to meet the needs of the agencies that commissioned them. In the early stages of my Post-Doctoral fellowship there was some similarity between my research graduate assistantship and the work I was doing. However, as I became more competent on the work that I was assigned, I became a trusted junior scholar and respected researcher. I was given equal voice on all matters in the department and was assigned to lead various projects. Beyond the academic development was the intimate exposure to the politics of higher education.

## Navigating the Politics of Higher Education

It is perhaps important to state that the concept of being a minority academic did little to affect my approach to learning and the pursuit of a doctoral degree. It was evident that there was a scarcity of minorities in the doctoral program that I was pursuing. In fact, it most of the classes I took in my program, I was the only Black student. Yet that had little or no effect on my need to succeed. I certainly was not was ignorant of the fact that there were many barriers to minorities succeeding in higher education. Specifically, the work of Vaughn (2007) explicates some of the challenges that Black males face in either qualifying for college or having been admitted, persisting through to earning degrees.

It is also easy to fall into the trap of believing the propaganda that is implied by the statistics that show that there are more Black men in prison that any other racial group (see Vaughn, 2007). Instead, I chose to ignore the negative stereotypes that can in fact become self-fulfilling prophecies and to focus on other minority role models who were successful in academics and in other spheres.

It is widely known in higher education that colleges are often cited for not hiring enough minority faculty members. Colleges and universities can and should do more to remove barriers to high performing prospects entering and thriving in the academy. As minorities think of careers in the academy, it is advisable to seek out trail-blazers in their fields of study or professions, for they are the people who will help them navigate the challenges of the academy. Yet, there are other barriers besides ethnicity that can impede a person's success in the academy. Wagner (2006) described the many pitfalls that can beset the success of inexperienced professors who seek to establish themselves in the academy. The author stated that some of the simplest, unconscious acts like saying the wrong things to the wrong people could affect the prospect of gaining tenure in tenure granting institutions. Additionally, many professors fail to earn tenure because they are not productive enough. People who fail to publish enough articles, or fail to offer service inside and outside the academy may not be recommended for tenure in places where these artifacts are valued. However, a person may do everything that he or she is expected to do, but failed to impress the committee that would make a decision about the professor's future in the academy.

One of the treasured outcomes of my Post-Doctoral fellowship is learning to navigate the politics of the academy. There are many issues in the academy that fall under the classification of organizational politics. Even though much of the internal fighting is not obvious to students, it is very prevalent in the university. At the time of writing this chapter I have worked in three different universities and organizational politics presents itself in different ways. According to Wagner (2006) there is much to fight about in the academy, but one of the most prevalent drivers of organizational politics is the power struggle between faculty and administration. Power struggles occur for reasons such as differences of opinion about the management of scarce resources, limited space, who has decision making powers as the two groups fight about turf boundaries.

The knowledge that I acquired about the inner working of the academy during my Post-Doctoral studies illuminated some of the errors that I made when I started the doctoral program. I had brought considerable corporate experience to the academy, but that mattered little to senior academics. I had to distinguish myself as a learner and researcher if I was to gain the respect of my mentors and peers. The corporate experienced I acquired needed to be bolstered with research and a demonstration of the competence to become a scholar. Many of the assumptions that I had about the academy were untrue. I soon learned that it was not how smart I was, but how well I was prepared for the marathon of the Ph.D. and the non-academic barriers to success. I also learned that my degree would be *awarded* and not earned in the conventional sense of an education. I needed to win the favor of a committee who would eventually become my peers. Needless to say, my corporate attitude did not always mesh well with the academic culture. Perhaps I alienated myself from some senior professors because of my unorthodox approaches. But during my Post-Doc experience I clarified some of those misunderstandings and built some new relationships.

I was now ready for the academy. I had demonstrated that I had the capacity to do high quality research, I exemplified myself as a teacher, and I reframed my thoughts about how I might be successful. Despite the many challenges that I confronted on my journey through my studies, the Post-Doctoral experience provided an opportunity for me to establish myself as an academic and scholar. Had I taken a job immediately after graduation, I would have been totally unprepared for the role I was expected to play. I surmise that I would have struggled through my first year learning expensive lessons that I otherwise navigated through one year of a Post-Doctoral fellowship.

*What is a Clinical Position?*
*By Annie Smith, Ph.D.*

The U.S. Department of Education reported that in 2007, 83% of full-time faculty with tenure were White, and only 5% were Black. This has a far reaching impact on lives in numerous ways with one of them being salaries. In 2007 professors earned about $98,000, associate professors earned almost $71,000, and instructors earned around $51,600. See Table 2.4. Colleges and universities have created non-tenure earning jobs termed *clinical positions*. Individuals are employed to perform clinical or administrative functions rather than generating research. Frequently, clinical employees are hired on an annual contract with an option for renewal. These positions are often not as stable as tenure-track jobs. Clinical faculty members are hired for teaching and service and not research or publications. Some clinical positions are designed to operate as staff positions with more administrative work and less flexible work hours. In many cases clinical faculty have similar benefits as their tenure counterparts. Table 4.1.

Table 4.1. Full-Time Instructional Faculty Salaries at Title IV Degree 9-month Average Salaries

| Professors | $98,020 |
|---|---|
| Associate Professors | $70,744 |
| Assistant Professors | $59,283 |
| Instructors | $51,633 |
| Lecturers | $51,552 |
| No Academic Rank | $51,966 |

Source: U.S. Department of Education

As college enrollment increases, clinical positions are becoming more common. Some institutions are trying to remove the negative stigma attached to these positions. But most of us in clinical positions know that change does not come easily. Oftentimes, those in tenure positions fail to see clinical faculty as equals. I have had tenure-track faculty treat me less than equal and a few have been downright condescending—surmising that my position gives me few academic rights to pursue scholarly activities. Numerous African Americans, even those in tenure-track positions, report working in a hostile environment at colleges and universities. For many Black females, colleagues tend to ignore, isolate, or alienate them.

Similar to adjunct positions, African Americans are better represented in this area. Many are hired by the institutions where they earned their doctorates or institutions in their communities. Some clinical employees use these positions as a stepping stone to launch tenure track careers. And while others manage to turn their positions into tenure careers, many African Americans have to leave those institutions before they can secure tenure positions.

Minority support organizations have discussed the idea of having colleges "grow their own professors." One rationale is that minorities present a different perspective from traditional White male professors and therefore, can add a unique perspective to research and academia. But thus far there have not been a significant number of African Americans benefiting from this idea. Still there are additional challenges that minority faculty and staff must overcome because of negative societal stereotypes and their impact.

## Administrative Positions

White males dominate leadership positions in the academia and those in tenured positions. Academic administrators manage the day-to-day activities and provide instructional leadership for the institutions. They also set standards and policies; design curricular and set policies to meet the standards and goals. In 2011 records show that out of approximately 411,430 school administrators, 110,360 worked in postsecondary institutions. Twenty percent of all school administrators were minorities and 11% were categorized as Black or African Americans. According to the U.S. Bureau of Labor Statistics, the most minority administrators are principals and assistant principals in elementary and secondary schools. In academia administrative jobs are numerous. The top level administrative jobs at colleges and universities are presidents, deans, associate and assistant deans, and in some institutions intern deans. These positions are made up of the individuals who have the power to make numerous decisions. In addition to presidents and deans, there are other administrative staff jobs ranging from directors of programs to academic advisors. Top-level administrators typically get 4 to 5 weeks of vacation a year as well as health and pension packages. The salaries range from $158,000 for chief academic officers to $54,931 for directors of student activities. See Table 3.4. According to the U.S. Bureau of Labor Statistics, administrative positions are expected to grow and the job opportunities are expected to be excellent.

Some ask why African Americans have more opportunities to pursue administrative positions as compared to teaching and research chances. There a several reasons for this; one is that typically, there are more administrative jobs. Then, there seems to be more effort to recruit and retain minorities in these positions. Also, there appears to be a more sinister reason: African Americans are viewed as being more capable of performing administrative duties than conducting empirical research. The research interests of many minorities in academia are often treated as less relevant, especially when those interests involve studies focused on African Americans and other minority participants. Administrative careers frequently provide more stability and more professional growth opportunities. Much of the past and even current research fails to include minority participant. Despite the advances in African American administrative hires, the salaries for minorities, especially Black females, are still lagging behind their White counterparts. But administration in academia seems to be a place where Blacks have more opportunities and are making better strides.

Table 4.2. Salaries of Postsecondary Academic Administrators 2008-2009 School Year

| Academic Deans | Salary | Other Administrators | Salary |
|---|---|---|---|
| Business | $150,000 | Chief Development | $141,712 |
| Arts and Sciences | $134,632 | Dean of Students | $88,280 |
| Graduate Programs | $130,000 | Director, Financial Aid | $74,261 |
| Education | $128,500 | Registrar | $71,764 |
| Nursing | $125,400 | Director, Student Activities | $54,931 |
| Health-related Professions | $120,980 | | |

Source: The U.S. Bureau of Labor Statistics

## Chapter Five

## African American Achievement Gap

### Higher Education and the African American Achievement Gap

Conservative estimates suggest that teacher attrition in public schools is costing the United States over $7.3 billion a year. Teacher turnover has increased by 50% over the last 15 years (National Commission of Teaching and American's Future, 2007). Colleges of education throughout the country prepare thousands of future teachers each year, and most of the students enter the profession with hopes of being effective educators and improving the lives of future students. Career decisions are important and teaching has long term and far reaching effects on numerous individuals and the nation. Without academically equipping students for the future, we put our financial future in jeopardy as well as our security. We know that most students choose education as a career for altruistic and intrinsic reasons, despite arguments that the profession attracts students who struggle academically. Most states have increased academic requirements for students enrolled in teaching programs in colleges of education. Most institutions are providing teacher candidates who are highly qualified and more prepared to be effective educators than in the recent past.

### Teacher Motivation

Perceptions and attitudes about student racial differences manifest themselves in numerous ways in educational settings. Racial attitudes research provides strong evidence that African American English and other stereotypes often stigmatize and negatively impact students' academic and social success. Consequently, teachers have a major impact on student success or failure in school. Teachers have implicit theories about intelligence, knowing, and learning, and studying these theories and beliefs is important in understanding how teachers perform their duties in the classroom, and how this thinking influences instructional strategies and goal orientation.

In 2009, I surveyed 325 university students to examine the motivations for choosing teaching as a career. I examined 1) the educational beliefs of university students enrolled in beginning education courses, 2) their beliefs about the qualities and characteristics of good teaching, 3) their plans for future careers, and 4) whether theses students' decision to consider education as a career is related to their GPA or prior academic status. There were 284 Caucasians, 34 African Americans, 4 Hispanics, 2 Native Americans, and 1 Asian. Seventy-six percent of the participants were females, which is typical of the pool of education majors. Overwhelmingly, the students expressed a passion and determination to be effective educators, through service to those in their charge. Students commented that it will be their responsibility to insure that all of their students are given opportunities to succeed. There were no significant differences in the reasons these students choose education as a career. Most believed the profession is socially worthwhile and important. Eighty-six percent of the participants said that they chose teaching because they had inspirational teachers, and 87% felt that they had the qualities it takes to become good teachers after. They were asked to identify characteristics they believe teachers need to be effective. They listed altruistic and intrinsic characteristics, and few of them listed extrinsic reasons, such as summers and holidays. See Table 5.1.

Table 5.1. Motivational Factors Influencing Teaching as a Career: Perceptions of University Students in Beginning Education Courses

| Participants | Characteristics of an Effective Teacher |
|---|---|
| 35 | *I think a good teacher should understand, dedicated, and enthusiastic about their subject area.* |
| 256 | *The characteristics of a good and effective teacher are willingness to teach, the patience if something doesn't go as planned, the desire to help children personally and academically, and a good teacher will want to be a stepping stone in a child's educational journey so that they can have the opportunity to impact a child's life in a positive way.* |
| 132 | *Effective teachers are inspirational, encouraging and demanding. Good teachers will expect you to perform at your best and pull that potential out of students.* |
| 305 | *I think patience is key, also always maintaining hope and encouragement for your students.* |
| 78 | *A teacher must also be a good learner. She needs to learn everything she can about her students and the way they learn and make sure that she never leaves any student out.* |
| 60 | *Understanding, Patience, Courteous, Kind, Responsible. Passionate* |

Source: Smith, 2009, Unpublished

None of the participants reported choosing education as a major because of low grade point averages or academic status. The participants' high school GPAs, ACT/SAT scores were not significantly lower or higher than students enrolled in other colleges at the university. They were about average. And while in college, these students express great passion and an internal desire and determination to be effective educators, what happens within the first five years of being in the profession? It appears to be more than just the reality of dealing with the students in their classrooms. Many novice teachers report a lack of supportive administrators and/or parental behaviors as reasons for leaving the profession.

Frequently, reports cite the brokenness of the education system and the demoralizing effect it has on minority students. Teachers' perceptions of and attitudes toward their students tend to affect not only how they interact with them, but also their expectations of students. These beliefs about student differences, whether positive or negative, play a major role in the lives of students in and outside of the school environment. Negative racial beliefs about racial differences have harmful effects on African American students.   African Americans, because of cultural dialect and other racial differences, is perhaps the most stigmatized race throughout school systems in this country. Preconceived beliefs about students' abilities based on race or gender are still affecting educational decisions–despite convincing research. Current research involving the human brain is reversing previous assumptions about IQ, in addition to other issues. It is now known that IQ is affected by the amount of schooling students receive; and given adequate resources and training, students do improve, even those labeled *special need students.* Today throughout American public schools, Black students are disproportionately placed in special education classroom, where many perform monotonous tasks that fail to stimulate their brains and their academic growth. Once place in lower level courses, African American students remain there until graduating or dropping out of school. Furthermore, Black students are not well-represented in gifted classes; in middle and high schools, they are not in AP classes or the more strenuous classes–robbing them of opportunities to develop and improve the vital critical and independent thinking skills often associated with these courses.

In 1972, the United States Government released what has become known as the "Marland Report," named for S.P. Marland, the U.S. Commissioner of Education. This report brought gifted education to the national forefront and indicated that three to five percent of the nation's children could be considered gifted, that schools were not meeting the educational needs of the gifted, that differential education for this group was not a high national priority, and that, as a result, gifted students could suffer psychological damage and permanent impairment of their abilities.

Consequently, the federal government started financially supporting gifted and talented programs; perhaps, more importantly, they established a federal definition of gifted and talented which was based on achievement or potential and broken down into six categories. The categories were: general intellectual ability, specific academic aptitude, creative or productive thinking, leadership ability, visual and performing arts, and psychomotor ability. This 1972 definition with its various adjustments provides the bases for gifted programs in many of today's school systems.

The next national report, while not specifically about gifted education per se, once again brought attention to gifted education. The 1983 *A Nation at Risk* report criticized the country for low standards, loss of academic focus, and loss of academic ground to other nations in educating students. It detailed the country's neglect of high academic standards and abandonment of top academic students.

In 1993 the U. S. Department of Education released the last report. *National Excellence: A Case for Developing America's Talent* indicated that America had a "quiet crisis" in educating talented learners. Of the numerous issues addressed, the report once again cautioned the country about international educational competition, especially in science and math. It claimed "only a small percentage of students are prepared for challenging college-level work. The highest achieving U. S. students fare poorly when compared with similar students in other nations." It also highlighted the country's ambivalence toward intellect, the importance of social/emotional issues, rural and urban school settings, and the challenges of identifying culturally diverse students. Additionally, the report recognized the limited role the federal government had played in the promotion of gifted education since the Marland Report.

There are some special programs designed to address the perceived shortcoming of traditional schooling for gifted students—and not many such programs for students not classified as such. Special summer and Saturday programs have developed over the last decade. These programs vary on many dimensions, including content, duration, purpose, and sponsorship. With the belief that programs outside of school are absolutely necessary, these programs offer the gifted more opportunities for independent inquiry, in-depth study, and accelerated learning. They offer a pace and challenge that are more suitable to most gifted learners. Additionally, they are designed to meet both the intellectual and social-emotional needs of the gifted participants. Some programs offer mentoring, job-shadowing, and internships.

Administrators who have limited funding for gifted programs allow only a small number of gifted students to be served; and parents whose children are being served fear that if disadvantaged students are included their children will be excluded, so they defend the status quo. One solution for the equity and elitism problems in schools is to offer fair, practical models for identification and programming, meet the academic needs of students in the regular classroom, and train teachers to help maximize cognitive, affective, and ethical potential in students.

## Professional Development Schools

It is important to examine the education research and strategies being used to improve student achievement. Today, the emerging research on instruction is often called teaching for understanding, which uses multiple means of collecting data, including curriculum, classroom processes, teachers' instructional planning, and the teachers' thinking and decision making during instruction. Research on professional development schools (PDS) has primarily focused on teacher candidates. One of the functions of professional development schools is to prepare knowledgeable and skillful beginning practitioners (Castle, Fox & Souder, 2006; Teitel, 2004). A common method used to assess the impact of this training is a comparative study of PDS and non-PDS teacher candidates (Fountain, 1997; Telese, 1996; Sandhotlz & Wasserman, 2001). There is growing support suggesting that PDS-based teacher preparation of student teachers produces educators who are more competent in areas of instruction, management, and assessment.

In a 2006 study, Castle, Fox and Souder compared 91 PDS and non-PDS elementary teacher candidates from two cohorts. The participants were required to have completed a bachelor's degree and have a minimum grade point average of 3.0. The admission requirements were the same for both PDS and non-PDS applicants, and participants were allowed to choose the program. PDS candidates, full-time students, had daytime courses and a year-long internship. Non-PDS candidates were part-time students with evening courses until the student teaching semester.

Assessment tools included student teaching evaluation forms and tapes of student teaching portfolio presentations. Using qualitative and quantitative analysis, researchers found that PDS candidates showed higher levels of ability to assess students using a variety of methods (e.g. observation, communicating with students about their progress, and a variety of assessment methods). Additionally, PDS-trained candidates scored higher on content accuracy and clear instructions as well as classroom management. Researchers concluded that these results indicate that PDS teacher candidates might be able to spend more time on instruction and less on classroom management than the non-PDS trained teacher candidates. These results indicate a need for "teacher preparation that is deliberate and systematic in building connectivity between schools and universities so that teacher candidates can build connectivity between theory and practice" (Castle, Fox, & Souder, 2006, p. 78).

Recently, more teacher candidate research has focused on empirical inquiry of candidate supervision with PDS teacher mentors. The PDS mentors are described as experienced teachers who engage in reflective practice and instructional supervision of teacher candidates over an extended period of time– typically one year. A study conducted by Yendol-Hoppey (2007) concluded that teacher education programs benefit when teacher mentors embrace their role as school-based educators. The school-based educator was conceptualized as allowing teacher educators to shape and conduct their own work with student teachers as opposed to university supervisors. Some studies track the changes in philosophy and attitudes of teacher candidates toward teaching by using survey questions before and after field experiences. Others, using a similar design, compare developmental stage differences utilizing a teacher needs assessment questionnaire of traditional pre-service teachers and PDS interns within a university's program (Runyan, Parks & Sagehorn, 2000). For the most part, these studies are based on self-report data using survey instruments and focus on self-perceptions of efficacy.

## PDS Collaborative Research

Teachers and university faculty are conducting collaborative PDS research designed to bring about renewal and restructuring of public schools. Two criticisms of educational studies, conducted by university researchers over the years, have been that the research is oftentimes irrelevant to practice and is not easily accessible to practitioners. Clearly, there are some noted obstacles in constructing collaborative research. First, the incentives for participation in collaborative research are different for teachers and university faculty. For university faculty the incentives may be potential publication, promotion, or tenure, and the teacher may feel like the "subject" of the research instead of an equal partner. Also, in some PDS partnerships, the university is viewed as a privileged partner, reaping the benefits of the research, which is often viewed as irrelevant and of little practical daily use to practitioners. Preferably, collaborative educational research should be conducted by both teachers and researchers focused on school-based questions. In contrast to traditional research where university faculty have the primary or sole responsibility for research topic and design, collaborative research provides public school personnel a more active role. Basically, all phases of the research are shared, although one party may have primary responsibility. At times when collaborative teams have conducted the research, there are few authors who have documented the impact of these studies. Documented PDS research conducted by collaborative teams is critical for the improvement of teaching and learning.

Researchers (Mebane & Galassi, 2003) investigated the effects of group and task variables on perceived team learning by public school and university participants. As a result, they documented the importance of group dynamics, group leadership, and group process. The participants consisted of school teachers and administrator and university faculty members and graduate students. The PDS consisted of book discussions, other school or program visitations, survey development, and within-school professional development presentations for professional growth. The participants selected their own areas for professional development. Both school and university facilitators with expertise were sought to conduct the sessions, but co-leadership was not always possible. Like similar studies, the findings show a high correlation between feelings of trust, being able to risk sharing thoughts and ideas, and perceived individual growth in the groups. Mebane and Galassi argued that PDS participants are not aware of the basic principles of group dynamics, and educators need to consider the unique characteristics of group participants, who are mostly school teachers. But none of this research matters

## No Child Left Behind

President George Bush signed NCLB into law in January 2002, teaching students critical thinking skills took a backseat, and standardized testing became the priority. The NCLB law contained the most sweeping education changes since the *Elementary and Secondary Act* first enacted in 1965. A major goal was to close the achievement gap, which is defined as the difference between how well low-income and minority children perform on standardized tests as compared with their peers. Some basic principles of the law are: stronger accountability for results, increased flexibility and local control, expanded options for parents, and emphasis on proven teaching methods. All students were required to participate in testing. If special needs students did not take the tests, it was counted against the schools. The premise of the law to close the achievement gap appeared to be a much needed first step; it was the implementation of the law that almost devastated education reform.

First, there was no funding to help states apply the required changes in school systems. It is understandable that the schools with fewer resources and in impoverished areas tend to encounter more challenges in helping students achieve academic success. Usually, it is harder to recruit and retain effective teachers to these schools; and many of the parents work more than one job or do not have the means to help their children succeed. However, the states did have the authority to implement their own plans for standardized testing.

Secondly, the accountability requirements did more harm than good for the students and the schools. Each school was required to make adequate yearly progress (AYP) using the same standards of academic achievement for all students, "continuous and substantial academic improvement" for all students, and include high school graduation rates. And if schools did not perform, there were penalties. These penalties ranged from public notification and creation of an improvement plan to a state takeover of the school. The states were given until the 2013-2014 school year to bring all students to proficiency in math and science—which is an enormous task and most schools were not even close to achieving in 2012.

In 2011 President Barack Obama announced that the U.S. Department of Education would be giving NCLB waivers to give more flexibility to states by allowing them to come up with innovative ways to prepare students to compete for future jobs. Many states have applied and received the waivers, while a few others have not. And it appears that for now we are in a holding pattern.

*Academic Identity*

In the summer of 2012, I conducted a study with a group of African American students on several factors, including academic identity as they participated in an enrichment program. The African American students felt confident in their academic abilities and future academic success. The participants consisted of 40% females and 60% males. The participants were upcoming 6th and 7th graders. The group represented 15% of the school population. The school is made up of approximately one hundred and two, African American 6th and 7th graders. Eighty-four percent of the students receive free lunch and 95% are eligible for subsidized lunch. The school is located in a small town, where the population was slightly above two thousand people with a median household income of approximately $26,554 in 2010. The 2010 census data show that 51% of the residents were White and 46.73% were African American.

The pilot enrichment program was designed with the coordinated efforts of researchers and the school administrators to provide academic, health, and cultural enrichment for the participants. The program focused on science, math, cultural pride, and health literacy. The science activities included analyzing science experiments, creating individual ecosystems, and an intense focus on scientific concepts based on national and state standards. The math activities emphasized written and verbal practice of math facts and operations as well as the incorporation of technology using games and researched-based remediation and enhancement programs. Daily discussions of African American contributions locally, statewide and nationally, field trips to museums and institutions highlighting African Americans struggles and achievements, a study of African dance and music, and a study of health issues through the creation of an individual health genealogy chart.

The University of Alabama provided funding for the teacher stipends, academic materials and supplies, field trips, and transportation. The school provided classroom space, science and computer labs, and daily lunches. Volunteers, a graduate assistant, and two university faculty planned and facilitated the health literacy activities, cultural education, and field trips.

During the two years prior to the summer program, the school focused on improving math, reading, and science scores. State testing of the group shows that the students are improving. The state test consisted of reading and mathematics and examined four levels of achievement: Level 1 (does not meet standards); Level II (partially meets standards); Level III (meets standards), and Level IV (exceeds standards). Academically, the participants' scores on state tests in math and reading illustrate the students are meeting the standards or exceeding them, overwhelmingly in math. See Figure 5.1. Eighty-three percent of the females and 31% of the males exceeded the standards in math.

Figure 5.1. State Testing Levels. Summer Enrichment 2012

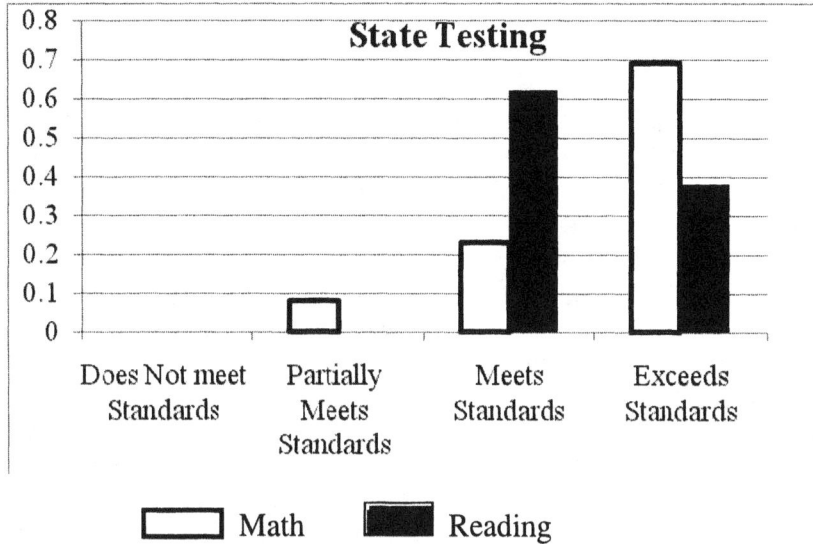

The students exhibited high *hope* and *self-efficacy.* The data show that there was correlation among the students' *school engagement, supportive relationships,* and individual *coping strategies.* More research is needed to evaluate the effectiveness of summer enrichment programs, particularly in low SES schools, where resources are limited and research is almost nonexistent. In this study, we were able to see small academic gains in a short period of time, implementing activities that have proven to be more student-centered and culturally- friendly. The long lasting effects are not always immediately evident because some changes are gradual. Research shows that the implemented activities of the summer enrichment program are key and crucial when working with students in schools with limited resources. The activities are similar to those that have shown to physically change the brain and are capable of increasing brain processing speed, memory, attention span, and sequencing skills. School administrators concur that a longer summer program would help students meet academic standards and encourage them to become lifelong learners. A year-round collaborative project focusing on cognition, health, identity, and culture will help the students become more invested in and motivated about their education and well-being.

It is not unusual for students of this age to still be engaged and motivated when it comes to school. It is when they get older that it tends to become harder to keep them academically motivated and in school. And for many students in impoverished areas, higher education is almost an impossible option.

The U.S. Education Department released a report from the 2009-2010 school year that should be a wakeup call for all of us. The report surveyed 72,000 schools, which serve 85% of American students. Astonishing but not surprising, African American students receive harsher disciple than their White peers, even in the same school systems. Black students made up 42% of the referrals schools made to law enforcement. These students made up only 18% of the sample, and yet 35% of African American students were suspended and 39% were expelled. Basically, African American students were three times as likely to be suspended as compared to non-minority students. Educators have known this disturbing trend for decades, and yet it keeps getting worse. When I was a high school teacher, a local reporter set off a major controversy when he revealed the alarming numbers of African American students getting discipline referrals in the district. He suggested that it was because the majority of the teachers were White females and were possibly afraid of Black students. My colleagues were livid; how could anyone even suggest racism or discrimination as a possibility, let alone discuss it as a valid hypothesis? Instead, one of my White colleagues referred to her African Americans students as *beasts*. Most of the teachers were not willing to examine the notion that a racial discussion was needed and options for discipline reflected upon and possibly revised. When the society as a whole views a group in negative terms, it can become a self-fulfilling prophecy and even members within the group will question whether or not the negative views are correct. This subject tends to be like discussions of race in this country; people are more comfortable ignoring the problems than to admit that it is a problem that should be addressed by considering many possibilities and finding the actual reasons why this is exists.

The great "White migration" from public to private schools during the 1960's and 70's set a precedence that still have effects on the education system. Then, many White parents were against school integration and believed as Alabama Governor George Wallace did in his 1963 inaugural address: "segregation today; segregation tomorrow; segregation forever." Today numerous White families, as well as some minority families, choose to send their children to private schools for several reasons, including hopes for a better education for their children.

The years before school integration were mired in educational inequality for African American students. Even after integration, most Black students had not been given the same resources as White students and were not as academically advanced. As unfair funding for poorer schools continues in this country, the more it seems as if little has changed to help improve the educational opportunities for minorities.

The stretched education budget provided by local and federal governments in many cases must also provide resources to private schools. Additionally, public schools in more affluent areas spend more money per pupil than in poorer neighborhoods which is populated more with minority students. Current research on poverty suggests that economic conditions impact the types of social skills and language that students develop; but also as a result, cognitive processes are hindered because of a lack of resources and availability to an appropriate and effective education. Such conditions impose a wide range of stressors on students, including issues of health, family instability and greater exposure to violence, and more limited extra-familial social support networks. The academic success of all students should be of great concern for all Americans. Policymakers should be especially concerned because of the future of the labor market with potential earnings and college successes are at stake. Ultimately, it benefits the country when more students are successful, academically. When more students are prepared for the workforce with higher level skills, the more they can contribute financially to society. They will become less dependent on others for support.

## Ability Grouping

Research and debates about ability grouping have pointed to the promise of providing quality instructional practices to all students, regardless of their perceived ability, ability-group, race or social class, to effectively increase student achievement for all (Loveless, 1999; Ross & Harrison, 1999). Traditionally, students are placed in ability groups based on intellectual ability measured through some combination of cognitive ability and IQ tests, academic achievement and/or teacher recommendations. Ability grouping takes different forms at different grade levels and varies by organizational dimensions across schools. Research indicates ability groups place a disproportionate number of low-income and minority students into lower-ability groups. Thus, ability grouping becomes a type of sorting mechanism for racial segregation, and appears to reinforce inequitable practices and negative stereotypes

(Oakes, Gamoran, & Page, 1992). One reason for the disproportionately high number of minority students in lower groups is consistently lower scores on achievement tests. Although cultural biases of test can be questioned, this finding in itself is not problematic. However, when students are placed in lower groups they receive less effective instruction. This serves only to place these students at a greater disadvantage. A second reason is stereotypical expectations that society and schools have of low-income and minority students. This is consistent with the finding that teachers' perceptions of appropriate student placement into various tracks and ability groups have a small, but significant, link to students' race, ethnicity, and social class.

As we examine possible causes for the achievement gap among the races, there are three likely scenarios that need to be examined: Is the problem cultural differences, stereotypes, or just bad behavior by African American students? First, are there noticeable cultural differences among Whites and African Americans? It is a fact that more minority students, e.g. African Americans, are put into special education programs and set on a track where they have little to no opportunities to receive effective academic opportunities and resources. There are cultural differences in how students learn, and yet this is not a major consideration in many school districts. Some would argue that the income differences tend to be more prevalent than the cultural ones. Most K-12 teachers are middle class, and increasingly more students are living in poverty. Essentially, there are structures in place which provide more and better resources to middle class families while discriminating against poor and/or minority students.

Secondly, once again stereotypes play a pertinent role in classrooms. Past gender stereotypes lead to female students being labeled as inept in math and possibly science. Males were said to be less proficient in reading and writing. Females were frequently steered toward writing and discouraged when it came to math proficiency. Typically, teachers gave males more time to solve math problems and even encouraged them to try harder to find answers. African American students were put in remedial or general education courses and more White students were put in accelerated and advanced placement courses. Because of lawsuits, some school systems began allowing high school students to choose their own courses regardless of recommendations from teachers and/or grade point averages. Somehow it doesn't seem ethical to deny students optimal settings for learning, particularly based solely on test scores and/or teacher recommendations.

All students deserve the right to an effective and fair education. Excluding students from programs which could potentially help them is totally unacceptable. Still, many African American students choose basic education courses instead of the more advanced and challenging courses when given a choice. As a high school teacher, I asked Black students why they didn't take the more challenging courses; many replied that the teachers were too hard and required too much work. The curricula in advanced classes tend to aid students in the development of critical thinking skills and usually allow students to participate in activities/experiments that will help them in college and in life. Usually, students in the more advanced classes have more academic success than students in the so called basic, regular, or general classes. Underachievement is a learned behavior and an important result when students are bored and/or not being challenged. Education plays such a major role in the lives of students. Statistically, students' academic success has a direct correlation to their economic and career success. With so much at stake, students should be given every chance to participate in educational programs that have the power to improve their potential for future success. How do we help African American students become more prepared to take these courses?

Lastly, we need to examine if African American students' behavior is worse than their White peers? As an educator for a couple of decades, I know that students will most often meet a teacher's expectations. Expect the best from all students and they will become more effective students. Now, I am a realist and know that there are circumstances in which students are faced with so many problems and situations that teachers have a limited effect on their academic progress.

I don't want to suggest the achievement gap lies solely on teachers. Not only is that unfair, but it is not even logical. Teachers have plenty of power in their roles, but they are not super human. In public schools teachers cannot choose the students they instruct. And so the students come with their problems— the physical, emotional, and social damage relatives and society have helped to cause. There are too many variables to take into account to argue that teachers are the primary factor for academic failure and the growing achievement gap.

## Self-regulated Learning

Definitions of self-regulation are numerous and highly complex but involve the development of automatic behaviors to facilitate personal development. Some believe that it has to be taught and controlled. If self-regulated learning has to be taught and does not come naturally, then how does one explain the people throughout history who were denied a formal education and yet became academic scholars in their own right? The politics of education has created a system whereby students are trained to become little clones of whatever theory is popular at the time. This, coupled with societal pressure for students to perform on standardized test, leaves little room for learners to develop self-regulatory abilities naturally.  I am somewhat torn between the belief that all children are born with the ability to self- regulate academically and the degree to which they can monitor themselves. On the one hand, I feel that there are those students who cannot develop academic self-regulatory strategies without some type of mediation whether it is the use of tools such as educational games, social interaction with peers, or the directed help of teachers. And then there are those born with the ability to somehow teach themselves self-regulation. Effortful control in academic achievement is fostered by students' abilities to maintain attention to succeed at academic tasks and to persistently work on that task in the midst of more appealing options. Children high in effortful control, among other characteristics, tend to have low levels of negative emotions and consequently high academic success.

Dr. Gloria Ladson-Billings, professor of urban education and acclaimed author, speaks of an "achievement debt" rather than an achievement gap. Her premise is that words have power and when we term it a gap, we lay total blame on the students. But defining it as a debt implies that society has shortchanged these students and therefore should provide them equal opportunities and adequate resources to help them succeed academically (2012). Numbers verify that African Americans students attend the most poverty-stricken schools and are expected to be able to compete with students who have, in some cases, 50% more resources and opportunities. There are those who argue that poor and/or minority students have few role models for good work ethics, when being poor takes more work than having wealth ever did. For most African Americans, having role models is not the major problem but having a system that is fair and equitable poses more of a challenge.

As an African American educator and researcher, I am especially disheartened by the widening achievement gap between Whites and

Blacks. There are various reasons suggested for the achievement gap, including socioeconomic and sociocultural status. However, recent findings that the achievement gap is not limited to lower SES in African American students, and findings that the achievement gap occurs before children begin school have caused researchers to look more deeply at the environments of African American families. Will this line of research reveal any revolutionary or even helpful information that will help African American students in academic settings? More research will help answer that question. However, it is a fact that more minority students, e.g. African Americans, are put into special education programs and set on a track where they have no to little opportunities to receive effective academic opportunities and resources. There are cultural differences in how students learn and yet this is not a major consideration in many school districts. And to me that does not constitute fairness or equity. Somehow it doesn't seem ethical to deny students optimal settings for learning, particularly based solely on test scores or teacher recommendations. All students deserve the right to an effective and fair education. Excluding students from programs which could potentially help them is totally unacceptable. I am afraid that the increased focus on test scores for all students will make education even less *student-oriented,* and the achievement gap between White and minority students will continue to widen.

Education plays such a major role in the lives of students. Statistically, students' academic success has a direct correlation to their economic and career success. With so much at stake, students should be given every chance to participate in educational programs that have the power to improve their potential for future success. Statistically, students' academic success has a direct correlation to their economic and career success. With so much at stake, students should be given every chance to participate in educational programs that have the power to improve their potential for future success. I feel that I can do more, and it is just a matter of figuring out the most effective strategies to make it happen.

## Impact of Minority Faculty

During my pursuit of 4 college degrees and listening to dozens of professors, I had two who were African American. Both were female; one was an adjunct instructor, and the other one was an associate professor. The professor had a doctorate in language arts education. I was getting my second degree in English education, so I took several of her classes. She was very knowledgeable, personable, but the fact that she was an African American female like me made the biggest impression on me. I didn't expect any more from her than I did any of my other professors. But I felt confident when I was in her classes. I cannot explain if fully, but I felt accepted, empowered, challenged and happy. I felt challenged because I didn't want to let her down. I assumed she had gone through a lot to become a professor, so I didn't want to embarrass her by not living up to my potential, especially in front of the other students. She was not my advisor nor did we know each other on a more personal level. But seeing her success inspired me to believe that one day I could become a university professor. Some of my African American friends expressed similar feelings about having a Black professor. I can only hope that when all of students see me in my role that they feel accepted and that they are comfortable enough to seek my help if needed. But there are still few African American professors compared to the number of students.

Today, the African American student enrollment in institutions of higher education is around 12%, while African American faculty hires are less than half of that number. There is evidence that African American faculty plays an important role on college campuses and the recruitment of minority student enrollment. Typically, the presence of Black faculty positively impacts efforts to recruit African American students to college campuses. They also offer students of all races different perspectives on racial and social issues which can prove valuable in an environment that focuses on knowledge and enlightenment. Minority faculty may be the only ones of their race students see in leadership roles. It is important for students in a nation that is made up of people from all races, cultures, and religious beliefs to know that academic success isn't limited to a select group nor is that success unattainable by African Americans. As minorities become the majority, what is the excuse for more sustained, credible efforts to recruit minority faculty, including African Americans.

I realize that the heart and soul of whom I am overwhelmingly reflect a desire to motivate students and help to support and empower teachers so that educating our children is a successful venture. Teachers have a major impact on student success or failure in school. Teachers have implicit theories about intelligence, knowing, and learning, and studying these theories and beliefs is important in understanding how teachers perform their duties in the classroom, and how this thinking influences instructional strategies and goal orientation. However, teachers cannot improve academic achievement without the help of ours.

# Chapter Six

# Next Steps

## Facing the Past

In 1968 I walked down a deserted dirt road surrounded by cotton fields on each side and a path of never-ending trees in the background. I anxiously anticipated the next day that would begin a new phase in, not only my life, but in the lives of thousands of people in the state of Mississippi. I was going to the 3$^{rd}$ grade in an integrated school in a small southern town–an event that would be repeated throughout school systems in the state. The weeks leading up to the day were filled with adults whispering and occasional debates about keeping us home for fear of the Whites retaliating for losing their bid to keep schools segregated. Prior attempts to integrate schools and universities were overshadowed with violence and even death. Southern Whites were adamant about keeping public schools segregated. During the late 60's and 70's, many Black students attended schools that were *separate and totally unequal—* old textbooks, fewer teachers, fewer resources, and less money.

At age 7, I wondered why they hated us so much. What was it about my skin color made me the enemy? My family had been forced to leave our home because they accused my grandfather of looking at a White woman; in the middle of the night we left to avoid harm. So I knew why my mother was afraid of letting me go to the school.

The next day we integrated schools. That first year saw several racial fights. The high school Black students refused to be spat on or called racial slurs without defending themselves. It was goodbye Dr. King and welcome Malcolm X. It was ironic that the Black students were the ones labeled violent and oftentimes punished when the Whites who started it were not. It is true that these events happened in the past, but these are things that are among the racial history of America that have not been discussed or confronted. Instead, we have been told to forget about the past. But it appears to be okay for southern Whites to keep the confederacy alive each year as they reenact war scenes, even though the fact that the South lost the Civil War will not get a "do over." Heritage not hate, right? The past is with us, and its effects are real.

In 2012 a Black man is in the White House. But how do we explain the racial tension that has elevated over the last 4 years? Do we blame it on fear? Maybe we blame it on a lack of acknowledgement that these events occurred and that racial discrimination continues today, and maybe a feeling that an acknowledgement will lead to unanticipated results that we as a country are not prepared to deal with or accept.

## The Barriers to Progress

Traditionally, the professoriate has been an environment of competition rather than cooperation. Competition is more challenging when, as a race, individuals have been excluded and denied equal opportunities to pursue certain careers. As a member of the faculty at a university, imagine being marginalized and told that your research interests should not focus on African Americans because it will be hard to publish. Imagine feeling invisible and isolated by virtue of your race in an environment, where there is an underrepresentation of minorities. Imagine being excluded and not invited to program meetings and having the department head tell you there is nothing he can do to get the program chair to include you in the meetings, where decisions about the program are made. These are just a few of the experiences African American faculty members report at postsecondary institutions. Blacks report receiving little guidance in the workplace and/or during the promotion process. They report less job satisfaction and limited opportunities to participate in departmental and institutional decision making. Indeed, there appears to be systematic structures in place that contribute to the continued underrepresentation of African Americans in higher education. Academia is often an environment that presents cultural barriers to change. One would think that this is still the 19th century and, change although inevitable, is slow to come. To be fair, some institutions are making tremendous progress in their efforts to recruit, support, and retain faculty, including those of color. It is beneficial to examine how far we have come in higher education post-Civil War.

The first African American to earn a Ph.D. from an American university was Edward Alexander Bouchet in 1876. He graduated from

Yale with a degree in physics. And although he was one of six people at the time to earn a degree in physics, he was denied the opportunity to conduct scientific research and achieve professional recognition simply because of his color. His grades and academic work were not in question (Mickens, 2002). The fact is, he was born into a segregated American society and despite his tremendous accomplishments, the American higher education system said, "you are not welcome because you are not one of us." His only option was to work in what was then called colored institutions. On the other hand, Patrick Francis Healy, who is credited with being the first African American to earn a Ph.D., seemed to have had more success breaking through the color barriers. Healy's father was a White Irish slave owner and mother was a Black slave, Haley earned his degree in 1865 from the University of Louvain in Belgium. He was the first person of African descent to become a president at a predominately White university (Foley, 1952).

Then in 1921 three African American women earned Ph.D.'s: Sadie Tanner Mossell Alexander, Georgiana Simpson, and Eva Beatrice Dykes. Alexander earned a doctorate in economics from the University of Pennsylvania. She is credited with several firsts as an African American woman, including the first to be admitted to and graduate from the Pennsylvania Law School. Alexander fought for civil rights for all (University of Pennsylvania Almanac, 2002). Georgiana Simpson earned a Ph.D. in German from the University of Chicago. Her interests in studying the German culture led to an investigation of her loyalty to the United States, but there was no evidence of any disloyalty. As a teacher, she felt that it was important to teach students the history of race relations and was passionate about her work (University of Chicago Libraries, n.d.). Eva Beatrice Dykes graduated from Radcliffe College with a degree in English. She was also a prolific writer, authoring several books and numerous articles. Dykes was a piano prodigy as a child (Bathurst, 1989). I truly appreciate the sacrifices and accomplishments of these and other individuals who didn't let racial and sexual discrimination defer them from changing the status quo and paving the way for others.

## Ownership

The student learning environment and quality teaching directly and indirectly affect student achievement. Classroom environments vary depending on the teacher as well as the student population which can be enhanced or hindered by teaching practices. Effective teaching is a complex, involved subject–one that cannot be summed up using one method to fit all teachers. Generally, people define effective teaching based on their personal classroom experiences, which can be different from person to person. A consistent, working definition of effective teaching has eluded researchers and educators for years. Learning is a complex process that individuals oftentimes exhibit unique characteristics. An added complicating factor is emotions. Emotions play a role in how some students learn.

Students have a basic cognitive need to feel competent and valued, which influences their feelings of self-worth. Positive feelings of self-worth can increase with successful experiences but challenging experiences can also help students realize individual growth opportunities or an awareness of personal limitations. In classroom settings and greater emphasis on standardized testing and increased accountability, students have fewer opportunities to develop personal and social development.

However, students and families need to take responsibility in the educational process and individual academic achievement. Students need to be aware of the importance of their education and be willing to take control of the aspects of it when possible. Every student has the right to an equal education and multiple individuals, and institutions have a responsibility to make it happen.

## *A New Generation*

Today, young people seem to be more inclusive and respectful of racial and cultural differences. As a graduate assistant, I conducted research on how high school students, Black, Caucasian, and Hispanic, construct an understanding of historical events using primary and secondary documents. One of the events was the infamous *stand in the schoolhouse door* by Governor George Wallace in his attempt to keep African Americans, Vivian Malone and James Hood, from being admitted to The University of Alabama. I showed the students several written accounts of the event: a newspaper article, a textbook, interviews with Jones and Hood, and the Governor's inaugural address. Then they were shown three photographs of the event: a newspaper photo of a federal marshal escorting Malone to Foster Auditorium, Wallace standing in the door of the auditorium, and the National Guard snipers on the roof of the building. The students were from Tuscaloosa, Alabama, where the incident occurred. Students from Alabama have a unique perspective to think about events of the Civil Rights Movement since they happened so close, and probably affected hundreds of families. This is particularly true about school desegregation; it is an event that occurred only a mile or two from where local students attend school. As part of the research, they read each document aloud and said whatever came to mind during the reading process. Each session was conducted individually, but the comments were similar. The students appeared to feel comfortable commenting on race relations then and now. Several commented on how they have walked passed Foster Auditorium and how they would now see it differently. They were surprised that Malone looked calm as she walked alongside the marshal to enter the auditorium. Many said they did not feel as if they would have been strong enough to stand up to that level of racism.. On the other hand, several students said they respected Wallace for acknowledging his mistake and apologizing for it.

Several White professors have said that when a Caucasian researcher or writer talks about racial discrimination against African Americans, it is more acceptable to the public than when a Black researcher or writer presents it. There is something seriously wrong with that reality. Most Blacks know and have lived discrimination and should be viewed as credible concerning this issue. There have been numerous studies and unfair laws documenting racism and inequality. We see it as African American males have been profiled for criminal behavior simply by being Black, and there are many other examples. I was somewhat dismayed when a friend of mine declined to give his input for this book project after agreeing to do so. His thoughts were that it could have negative consequences for his career. He was recently hired at a university in an administrative position after being an assistant professor shortly after earning his doctorate. According to him, his new employers would not be happy with the book claims of racial discrimination in higher education. After all, he made it and therefore, discrimination must not exist, right? Wrong! I have two thoughts about that. First, we work in higher education which supposedly embodies diverse perspectives, knowledge, enlightenment, and a degree of intellectual freedom. If we cannot have this discussion in higher education, how can we possibly expect to have it in any other settings? Second, if African Americans who have been successful in mastering a broad set of skills, expertise, and cognitive ability cannot share those perspectives and beliefs, what has been accomplished and at what expense? Until we can discuss these issues, civilly and respectfully of individual experiences and viewpoints, we will continue to hinder this country's ability to positively grow and become more prosperous, financially, socially, and emotionally.

# References

Aronson, E. (2004). The social animal. New York, NY: Worth.

Asher, J. W (2003). "The rise to prominence: Educational psychology 1920-1960." In B.J. Zimmerman & D.H. Schunk (Eds.), *Educational Psychology: a Century of Contributions.* Mahwah, NJ: Lawrence Erlbaum Associates.

Bandura, A. (1977). "Self-efficacy: Toward a unifying theory of behavioral change." *Psychological Review,* 84, 191-215.

Bathurst, D.B. (1989). *Eva Dykes: A star to Show the Way.* Writers Consortium Books

Brown, D.L. & Tylka, T.L. (2010). "Racial Discrimination and Resilience in African American Young Adults: Examining Racial Socialization as a Moderator." *Journal of Black Psychology.* Retrieved from http://www.sagepublications.com

Bureau of Labor Statistics. (2012). *Education administrators.* Retrieved from www.bls.gov.oco/ocos007.htm

Castle, S., Fox, R., & Souder, K. (2006). "Do Professional Development schools (PDSs) Make a difference? A Comparative Study of PDS and Non-PDS Teacher Candidates." *Journal of Teacher Education,* 57, 65-80.

Castle, S., Fox, R., & Souder, K. (2003). "Aspects of Teacher Quality in PDS and non-PDS Candidates." Report Submitted to the National Education Association PDS Research project.

Chavez, A.F. & Guido-DiBrito, F. (1999). "Racial and Ethnic Identity and Development." *New Directions for Adult and Continuing Education,* 84. 39-47.

Civil Rights Coalition (2002). "The voice of sanity about race and civil rights." New York, NY: Civil Rights Coalition. Electronic Version.

Clark, K.B., & Clark, M.P. (1950). "Emotional Factors in Racial Identification and Preference in Negro Children." *Journal of Negro Education,* 19, 341-350.

Cornbleth, C. (1988). "Curriculum in and Out of Context." *Journal of Curriculum and Supervision.* 3(2), 85-96.

Cornbleth, C. & Gottlieb, E. E. (1989). "Reform Discourse and Curriculum Reform." *Educational Foundations.* 3(3), 63-78.

Cross, W.E. (1971). "Negro-to-Black Conversion Experience." *Black World,* 20 (9), 13-27.

DuBois, W.E.B. (1903). *The Souls of Black Folk.* Chicago: A.C.: McClurg.

Eccles, J.S., & Wigfield, A. (1995). "In the Mind of the Actor: The Structure of Adolescents' Achievement Values and Expectancy-related Beliefs." *Personality and Social Psychology Bulletin,* 21, 215-225.

Eccles, J.S., Midgley, C., Wigfield, A., Miller Buchanan, C., Reuman, D., Flanagan, C., & MacIver, D. (1993). "Development During Adolescence: The Impact of Stage-Environment Fit on Young Adolescents' Experiences in Schools and in Families." *American Psychologist,* 48, 90-101.

Feistritzer, C.E. (2011). "Profile of Teachers in the U.S. 2011." Washington, D.C.: National Center for Education Information.

Ferguson, G.O. (1916). "The psychology of the Negro." Columbia University. Retrieved from http://www.archive.org/stream/psychologyofnegr00fergrich#page/n5/mode/2up

Foley, A.S. (1976). "Dream of an Outcaste: Patrick F. Healy: the Story of the Slave born Georgian Who Became the Second Founder of America's First Great Catholic University, Georgetown." Tuscaloosa, AL: Portals Press.

Gaines, S.O. & Reed, E. (1994). "Two Social Psychologies of Prejudice: Gordon W. Allport, W.E.B. DuBois, and the Legacy of Booker T. Washington." *Journal of Black Psychology,* 20, 8-28.

Galassi, J. P., White, K. P., Vesilind, E.M., Bryan, M.E. (2001). "Perceptions of Research from a Second-year, Multisite Professional Development Schools Partnership." *The Journal of Educational Research,* 95, 75-83.

Garrett, H.E. (1963). "Misuses of Overlap in Racial Comparisons." *The Mankind Quarterly.* Retrieved from http://www.unz.org/Pub/MankindQuarterly-1963apr-00254?View=PDF

Greenwald A., McGhee, D., & Schwartz, J. (1998). "Measuring Individual Differences in Implicit Cognition: the Implicit

Associations." *Journal of Personality and Social Psychology,* 74(6).

Hernstein, R.J. & Murray, C. (1994). *The BellCcurve: Intelligence and Class Structure in American Life.* New York, NY: Free Press Paperbacks

.Holmes Group (1986). *Tomorrow's Teachers: A Report of the Holmes Group.* East Lansing, MI: Author.

(---) (1990). *Tomorrow's schools: A report of the Holmes Group.* East Lansing, MI: Author.

Horowitz, R. (1936). "The Development of Attitude Toward the Negro." *Archives of Psychology, 104. Integrating the Life of the Mind: African Americans at the University of Chicago 1870-1940.* Retrieved from www.lib.uchicago.edu

Kozulin, A., Boris, G., Ageyev, V.S., & Miller, S.M. (Eds.). (2003). *Vygotsky's Educational Theory in Cultural Context.* New York, NY: Cambridge University Press.

Ladson-Billings, G. Julie C. Laible Memorial Lecture on Anti-racist scholarship, Education, and Social Activism. February 16, 2012. AL: University of Alabama..

*The Life and Accomplishments of Sadie Tanner Mossell Alexander.* (2002). University of Pennsylvania Almanac. 49(2).

Loveless, T. *The Tracking Wars. State Reform Meets School Policy.* Washington D.C.: Brookings Institution Press.

Maddux, J.E. (1995). *Self-efficacy, Adaptation and Adjustment: Theory, Research, and Application.* New York, NY: Plenum Press.

Marks, B, Settles, I.H., Cooke, D.Y., Morgan, L. & Sellers, R.M. (2004). "African American Racial Identity: A Review of Contemporary Models and Measures." In R.L. Jones (Ed.), *Black Psychology,* (4th ed.). Hampton, VA: Cobb & Henry.

Mebane, D.J., & Galassi, J.P. (2003). "Variables Affecting Collaborative Research and Learning in a Professional Development School Partnership." *The Journal of Educational Research.* 96, 259-268.

Metcalf-Turner, P. & Fischetti, J. (1996). "Professional Development Schools: Persisting Questions and Lessons Learned." *Journal of Teacher Education,* 47 (4), 292-299.

Mickerns, R.E. (Ed). (2002). *Edward Bouchet: The First African American Doctorate.* River Edge, NJ: World Scientific.

National Center for Education Statistics. (2009). Retrieved from http://nces.ed.gov/

National Science Foundation. (2009). Earned Doctoral Degrees. Retrieved                                                                              from

http://search.nsf.gov/search?access=p&output=xml_no_dtd&sort
=date%3AD%3AL%3Ad1&ie=UTF-
8&btnG=Google+Search&client=NSF&oe=UTF-
8&proxystylesheet=NSF2&site=NSF&q=doctoral+degrees

Oakes, J.A, Gamoran, & Page, R.N. (1992). "Curriculum Differentiation: Opportunities, Outcomes and Meanings." In P.W. Jackson (Ed.), *Handbook of Research on Curriculum.* Washington, DC: American Educational Research Association.

Parham, T.A. (1989). "Cycles of Psychological Nigrescence." *The Counseling Psychologist, 17,* 187-226.

Phinney, J.S. (1992). "The Multigroup Ethnic Identity Measure: A New Scale for Use with Diverse Groups." *Journal of Adolescence Research, 7,* 156-172.

Reed, C.J., Kochan, F.K., Ross, & Kunckel, R.C. (2001). "Designing Evaluation Systems to Inform, Reform, and Transform Professional Development Schools." *Journal of Curriculum and Supervision, 16,* 188-205.

Ross, C.M., & Harrison, P.L. "Ability grouping." In G. Bear, K. Minke & A. Thomas (Eds.), *Children's Needs II: Development, Problems and Alternatives.* Washington DC: National Association of School Psychologists, 1999.

Sandholtz, J. & Wasserman, K. (2001). "Student and Cooperating Teachers: Contrasting Experiences in Teacher Preparation Programs." *Action in Teacher Education, 23,* 54-65.

Sellers, R.M., Copeland-Linder, N., Martin, P.P., & Lewis, R.L. (2006). "Racial Identity Matters: the Relationship Between Racial Discrimination and Psychological Functioning in African American Adolescents." *Journal of Research on Adolescence, 16,* 187-216.

Sellers, R.M., Smith, M.A., Shelton, J.N., Rowley, S.A., Chavous, T.M. (1998). "Multidimensional Model of Racial Identity: A Reconceptualization of African American Racial Identity." *Personality and Social Psychology Review, 2,* 18-39.

Steele, C.M. (1995). "Stereotype Threat and Intellectual Test Performance of African Americans." *Journal of Personality and Social Psychology, 69,* 797-811.

Tatum, B.D. (2003). *Why are all the Black kids sitting together in the cafeteria?: And other Conversations about race.* New York: NY. BasicBooks.

Teitel, Lee (2001). "An Assessment Framework for Professional Development Schools: A Literature Review". In M. Levine

(Ed.), *Designing standards that work for professional development schools.* Washington, DC: National Council for Accreditation of Teacher Education. 33-79.

U.S. Department of Education. (2011). "Higher education." Retrieved from http://www2.ed.gov/about/offices/list/opepd/ppss/reports.html#h igher

Vaughn, E.L. (2007). "The Challenges of Retaining the African-American Male in Higher Education." MS: Alcorn State University. Retrieved 1/16/2012 from http://www.maricopa.edu/studentaffairs/minoritymales/TheChall angesofRetainingAAMales[1].pdf

Valli, L., Cooper, D., & Frankes, L. (1997). "Professional Development Schools and Equity: A Critical Analysis of Rhetoric and Research." In M. W. Apple (Ed.), *Review of Research in Education*, 22, 251-304.

Vygotsky, L.S. (1978). *Mind in Society.* Cambridge, MA: Harvard University Press.

Wagner, N.R. ( 2006)." Getting Tenure at a University." TX: San Antonio. http://cs.utsa.edu/~wagner/creative_writing/tenure.pdf

Wong, C.A., Eccles, J.S., & Sameroff, A. (2003). "The Influence of Ethnic Discrimination and Ethnic Identification on African-American Adolescents' School and Socio-emotional Adjustment." *Journal of Personality,* 71, 1197-1232.

Yendol-Hoppey, D. (2007). "Mentor Teachers' Work with Prospective Teachers in a Newly formed Professional Development School: Two Illustrations." *Teachers College Record,* 109, 669-698.

*Index*

www.ingramcontent.com/pod-product-compliance
Lightning Source LLC
Chambersburg PA
CBHW062043270326
41929CB00014B/2529